D0225021

THE BIRTH OF INDUSTRIAL BRITAIN

The Birth of Industrial Britain: Economic Change 1750–1850

KENNETH MORGAN

LONGMAN
LONDON AND NEW YORK

Addison Wesley Longman Limited,
Edinburgh Gate,
Harlow,
Essex CM20 2JE,
United Kingdom
and Associated Companies throughout the world.

*Published in the United States of America
by Addison Wesley Longman Inc, New York*

© Addison Wesley Longman Limited 1999

The right of Kenneth Morgan to be identified as the author
of this work has been asserted by him in accordance with
the Copyright, Designs and Patents Act 1988.

All rights reserved; no part of this publication may be
reproduced, stored in a retrieval system, or transmitted
in any form or by any means, electronic, mechanical,   ·
photocopying, recording, or otherwise without either the
prior written permission of the Publishers or a licence
permitting restricted copying in the United Kingdom
issued by the Copyright Licensing Agency Ltd.,
90 Tottenham Court Road, London, W1P 9HE.

First published 1999

ISBN 0-582-29833 4 PPR

Visit Addison Wesley Longman on the world wide web at http://www.awl-he.com

British Library Cataloguing-in-Publication Data
A catalogue record for this book is available from the British Library

Library of Congress Cataloging-in-Publication Data
Morgan, Kenneth.
  The birth of industrial Britain: economic change 1750–1850/
Kenneth Morgan
        p. cm. -- (Seminar studies in history)
    Includes bibliographical references and index.
    ISBN 0-582-29833-6
    1. Great Britain--Economic conditions--1760–1860.
  2. Industrialization--Great Britain--History.   3. Industries--Great Britain
  Britain--History.   I. Title.   II. Series
  HC254.5.M635   1999
  330.941--dc21   98-42241
                                                   CIP

Set by 7 in 10/12 Sabon
Printed in Malaysia. PP

CONTENTS

AN INTRODUCTION TO THE SERIES

Such is the pace of historical enquiry in the modern world that there is an ever-widening gap between the specialist article or monograph, incorporating the results of current research, and general surveys, which inevitably become out of date. *Seminar Studies in History* are designed to bridge this gap. The series was founded by Patrick Richardson in 1966 and his aim was to cover major themes in British, European and World history. Between 1980 and 1996 Roger Lockyer continued his work, before handing the editorship over to Clive Emsley and Gordon Martel. Clive Emsley is Professor of History at the Open University, while Gordon Martel is Professor of International History at the University of Northern British Columbia, Canada and Senior Research Fellow at De Montfort University.

All the books are written by experts in their field who are not only familiar with the latest research but have often contributed to it. They are frequently revised, in order to take account of new information and interpretations. They provide a selection of documents to illustrate major themes and provoke discussion, and also a guide to further reading. The aim of *Seminar Studies* is to clarify complex issues without over-simplifying them, and to stimulate readers into deepening their knowledge and understanding of major themes and topics.

NOTE ON REFERENCING SYSTEM

Readers should note that numbers in square brackets [5] refer them to the corresponding entry in the Bibliography at the end of the book (specific page numbers are given in italics). A number in square brackets preceded by *Doc.* [*Doc.* 5] refers readers to the corresponding item in the Documents section which follows the main text. Words and abbreviations asterisked at first occurrence are defined in the Glossary.

ACKNOWLEDGEMENTS

I have learnt much from teaching the Industrial Revolution, and am grateful to the pupils who have contributed to discussions on this topic at several educational institutions where I have taught: at Hyde Sixth Form College, Cheshire; at the now defunct West London Institute of Higher Education; and at my current academic base, Brunel University. I would also like to acknowledge the personal support offered by Leigh and Ross.

The publishers would like to thank the following for permission to reproduce copyright material:

'Document on Credit and the Cargo Trade' pp. 156–7 from *Capital and Credit in British Overseas Trade* by Jacob M. Price. Copyright © 1980 by the President and Fellows of Harvard College. Reprinted by permission of Harvard University Press; an extract from *Fisher Row, Fishermen, Bargemen, and the Canal Boatmen in Oxford, 1500–1900* by Mary Prior, pp. 364–5, copyright 1982, by permission of Oxford University Press.

PART ONE: THE BACKGROUND

1   THE BIRTH OF INDUSTRIAL BRITAIN

The purpose of this book is to introduce readers to the significance and scale of the economic changes in Britain throughout the century after 1750, while taking account of the older practices that persisted alongside the new. In doing so, we shall be investigating a much-debated tranche of history, for the Industrial Revolution has inspired many hypotheses and counter-theories about its extent and nature, with scholars often writing in close synchronization with readily identifiable features of their own social and economic setting [19]. As far as possible within the compass of a small textbook, differences between the early process of industrialization in England and Wales on the one hand and in Scotland on the other will be addressed. Since Britain was the first Western country to undergo an industrial revolution, the findings of this book have implications for students of industrialization in other contexts in time and space. The text is written for those with no previous detailed knowledge of Britain's early industrial economy and for those who need an overview of modern economic historians' findings on the subject. Statistics are deliberately woven into the text rather than presented as tables or appendices, for reasons of space but also to preserve readability in an introductory account.

The century covered in this book was the most important watershed in the economic and social development of Britain, for it witnessed the beginning of the process that we term the Industrial Revolution. Contemporaries were aware of the economic changes surrounding them, as travel accounts lauding the impact of canals, factories, docks, railways and agricultural improvement attest [e.g.12]. But important commentators such as Adam Smith and David Ricardo did not use the phrase 'industrialization'; the term 'industrial revolution' was not coined until the Frenchman Blanqui used it in the 1820s. The fact that contemporary descriptions refer extensively to changes in the industrial and agrarian landscape and yet shy away from the term industrial revolution implies that the dramatic economic and social changes only comprised the birth of industrial Britain in this period; hence the title of this book. The fully-fledged industrial, urban economy that saw Britain as the 'workshop of the world' did not occur until the mid-Victorian era.

ECONOMIC ADVANCE BY 1750

The early industrial revolution in Britain did not emerge in a vacuum. By 1750 England, and to a lesser extent Scotland and Wales, already had a social and economic situation conducive to industrialization. Britain's relatively small land mass, interspersed with navigable rivers, had the potential for transport development, for inter-regional flows of business, and for integration of a national economy. During the sixteenth and seventeenth centuries, England's economic position had been strengthened by the growth of widespread commercial agriculture rather than subsistence farming, by colonial and trade expansion across the Atlantic in particular, by the growth of rural manufacturing, and by relative political stability (save for the Civil Wars and Interregnum) compared with the religious strife of much of Europe [38]. Public credit had been placed on a sound footing by the creation of the Bank of England in 1694 and by the efficient handling of the National Debt. Government borrowing helped Britain wage war effectively against her main rivals, the Spanish and the French. The protection afforded by the Royal Navy for British foreign trade and colonial possessions also pointed to British economic and military power.

At home, significant economic advance had already been made by 1750. The leading river systems were made more navigable by improvements brought about by certain Acts of Parliament. Turnpike roads began to improve travel on the highways. Agricultural progress in the use of fodder crops and rotation of crops had begun. A capitalist putting-out system of production existed in some branches of the woollen industry. Technological improvements, notably the steam engine and the smelting of iron with coke rather than charcoal, were beginning to make an impact on industrial production. The leading outports were increasing the volume and value of their shipping and trade and encroaching on London's relative share of overseas commerce. The domestic market grew markedly as income per head of population expanded and a 'consumer revolution' percolated down from the richer classes to the middle ranks and artisans [40, 184]. Moreover, England had a more developed manufacturing sector amongst a predominantly rural population than was the case in France or Holland. None of these improvements was sufficient to cause an industrial revolution; but without the solid economic platform they offered already by 1750, British industrialization would have taken much longer than it did.

ECONOMIC GROWTH AFTER 1750

In designating the century after 1750 as the birth of industrial Britain, it is logical to enquire about the conceptual and empirical justification for such a description. Conceptually, early industrialization was the period of British history when there was a structural change in the economy from a predominantly rural, agricultural setting, with some manufacturing and trade and modest rates of population and economic growth, to a more urbanized, industrial country with a significant demographic upsurge and annual rates of economic growth of about 2 to 3 per cent. Thirty years ago it was fashionable to depict this transition as a short, sharp shock: various historians deployed statistical indicators to suggest that economic discontinuity occurred towards the end of the American Revolution and was particularly marked in the last two decades of the eighteenth century. The most famous advocate of this approach was W. W. Rostow, who argued that there was a 'take-off' in the British economy around 1780 linked with the swiftly emerging cotton industry as the leading sector of industry, which had multiplier effects* on other parts of the economy [47, 48].

Modern estimates of economic growth have smoothed out the path towards industrialization and discounted notions of radical discontinuity in the statistical indices around 1780; and it has been argued convincingly that growth rates for British industry do not bear out the prominence given to cotton above other industries. The historian mainly responsible for these data is N.F.R. Crafts. His projections of British economic growth indicate that national output reached the threshold that economists consider necessary for industrialization to occur, but that they did so more slowly and smoothly than historians accepted thirty years ago. Crafts's estimates reckon that annual national output grew slowly at a rate of 0.69 per cent in the first sixty years of the eighteenth century; remained at this level (0.70 per cent, to be exact) in the period 1760–80; climbed to 1.32 per cent in the years 1780–1801; and rose further at a rate of 1.97 per cent between 1801 and 1831 [20]. (It is worth pointing out that previously accepted estimates by Phyllis Deane and W. A. Cole projected an annual rate of 3.06 per cent for the latter time period [23].) Crafts's annual estimates for industry show a more accelerated rise: 0.71 per cent between 1700 and 1760; 1.51 per cent from 1760 to 1780; 2.11

per cent in the period 1780–1801; and 3.0 per cent from 1801 to 1831. Sectoral growth rates of real output varied in different industries, but what stands out for the entire period of Hanoverian Britain is the overall rise in most industries, not just cotton [20].

These estimates of economic growth are based on data that are problematic in their gaps and national coverage, and recently the difficulties of enumerating the Industrial Revolution have been exposed. Quantitative data are relatively poor for the industrial, service and agricultural sectors and often one has to overcome a 'meagre and mutilated' statistical record [31]. Moreover, some historians regard focus on these statistical indices as dehumanizing the Industrial Revolution, which was after all created by the efforts of people, the estimates of output merely being the summary outcome. There is, in fact, a danger that concentration on figures for economic growth can deflect attention from the regional nature of industrialization and from the important contribution of women and children's work in industry: both of these, it could be argued, were crucial features of raising productivity within the economy but both tend to be invisible in national growth indices [18]. Of course, the national data do hide the impact of regional industrialization; and many employment figures exclude female and child labour. Yet it is unrealistic to suggest that the estimates of real national output should be abandoned: without the quantitative rigour imparted by such figures, the timing and scale of industrialization would be difficult to demonstrate [43]. What is needed is a judicious intermixture of the growth rates to provide the broad parameters of the discussion, and the marshalling of further quantitative and qualitative evidence to substantiate or qualify the national accounts. This is the approach followed in this book.

PART TWO: ANALYSIS

2   POPULATION GROWTH

The growth of the early industrial economy in England was accompanied by a significant increase in population, and any understanding of economic and social development over the century after 1750 must take account of this demographic* change. The records for reconstructing population were purely local before 1800; they consist mainly of Anglican parish registers that record baptisms, marriages and burials. With the coming of the first census in 1801, there are more accurate measurements made every decade until today. Our understanding of population trends in recent years has been transformed by intensive work on these sources by the followers of the Cambridge Group for the History of Population and Social Structure under the leadership of E. A. Wrigley and R. S. Schofield [68, 69]. Allowing for the biases in Anglican parish registers, estimating data for the non-Anglican population, and using sophisticated computer techniques to facilitate back-projection* from the 1871 census and family reconstitution*, the Cambridge Group has produced estimates from which an analysis of demographic development can proceed. It cannot be emphasized too strongly that population figures published before the 1980s are seriously outdated, though older discussions of demographic change still offer some intelligent commentary. The following discussion is based mainly on material for England. Good demographic data for Scotland and Wales is less easily available, and investigation of the population history of those countries has been less sophisticated.

The statistical findings of the new research into demographic history can be set out first to provide a basis for analysis. The population of England was fairly static for the first half of the eighteenth century, but it then grew from 5.7 million in 1751 to 8.7 million in 1801 to 16.8 million by 1851. Scotland and Wales also experienced demographic growth, but not at quite so high a rate: the population of Scotland rose from 1.25 million in 1751 to 2.89 million a century later, while that of Wales increased over the same time-period from 0.45 to 1.2 million. From the 1780s until the outbreak of the First World War the English population was increasing by more than 10 per cent per decade, the fastest demographic growth in modern British history. The population continued to grow beyond the mid-Victorian period, but at a lower rate of increase. Urbanization spread rapidly with the growth of population. By 1801 London, with 959,000 inhabitants, was easily the largest city in Britain; there were fifteen towns in England and Wales with more than 20,000 people. By 1851, sixty-three towns had reached the latter threshold and London's population was 2.3 million. Among the rapidly growing urban centres were industrial cities such as Liverpool, Leeds, Sheffield, Birmingham and Manchester.

During the period of rapid demographic growth, the mean age of first marriage and the proportion of the population never marrying both dropped. In the period 1700–49 the mean age of first marriage for men was 27.5 years and for women, 26.2 years. These were comparatively late ages of marriage in western Europe at the time [59]. By 1800–49 the mean age of marriage had fallen for both sexes: to 25.3 years for men and to 23.4 years for women. Correspondingly, more people chose to marry. Fully a quarter of the population aged under 45 never married in the late seventeenth century; this proportion fell to 7 per cent in the second half of the eighteenth century.

Estimates of fertility* and mortality* produced by the Cambridge Group also reveal striking trends. Crude death rates in England and Wales fell from 26 per thousand in the 1750s to 22 per thousand a century later, with most of the decline coming after 1800. This fall was more impressive than these figures suggest because the urban death rate was normally higher than that in rural areas and so savings in mortality were achieved as the country became more urbanized. A fall in death rates led, of course, to a rise in life expectancy, even allowing for infant mortality. Most people born in England and Wales in the 1750s could expect to live for 36 or 37 years. A significant increase did not occur until well into the nineteenth century. By the 1850s, life expectancy reached 40 years of age. Trends in fertility resulted from changes in legitimate and illegitimate birth rates. Both rose in the century after 1750. Illegitimate fertility (or bastardy rates) rose from 2 per cent of all births in the late seventeenth century to 6 per cent after 1800. Legitimate fertility increased from 34 births per thousand of population in 1751 to a peak of 41 per thousand in 1821 and then tailed off to 36 per thousand in 1851 – remembering, of course, that the total population increased significantly over this period [67].

EMIGRATION AND IMMIGRATION

Analysis of these data must focus on the reasons for the increase in population and place them within their economic and social context. There are three broad ways of interpreting the findings. The first is to consider the impact of emigration and immigration upon the population totals. Clearly an influx or an exodus of people could have affected the overall figures. In this particular context, however, it is not a significant factor, for we know beyond doubt that emigration was not an important variable with regard to population size: between 1781 and 1851 net out-migration amounted to less than one in every one thousand inhabitants [68]. This means that demographic growth in England's early Industrial Revolution must have been triggered either by mortality or fertility or by a combination of the two rather than by emigration or immigration.

In looking at the reasons for trends in birth and death rates, some explanations are still speculative and the recent gains in our demographic knowledge have not yet led to full data on the regional dimensions of population change. Yet some overall contours can be presented that reflect the current state of research in a historical field which in the past twenty years has undergone more of a sea change in extending our knowledge than any other aspect of British social and economic history.

MALTHUS AND DEMOGRAPHIC THEORY

Discussion of mortality and fertility is greatly aided by the work of the Revd. Thomas Malthus, a pioneer demographer. A skilled statistician in touch with fellow political economists, Malthus was the first major British social scientist. In *An Essay on the Principle of Population*, written in 1798 and revised in 1803, he theorized that population growth and decline were linked to preventive and positive checks [*Doc. 1*]. By preventive check, Malthus referred to the constraints on fertility caused by moral restraint within marriage at a time when contraceptive techniques were primitive; he did not allow for controls on fertility in his model. Malthus's positive check was mortality, which he associated with misery and vice. In outlining the preventive and positive checks to population growth, he took account of the connections between the size of population and various economic and social factors. Trends in population, in his view, were closely related to rational decisions about marriage and conception of children made by individuals according to their economic circumstances. Malthus also argued that demographic growth must be considered in relation to food resources; populations grow geometrically (1, 2, 4, 8, 16, and so on) whereas food supplies can only increase at a lower pace, arithmetically (1, 2, 3, 4, etc.). Thus in cases where population size outstrips food resources, as in many of the developing countries of the world today, the result is sometimes referred to as a Malthusian crisis.

According to Malthus's positive check, the growth of a population would lead to higher food prices, which in turn would lower real incomes and result in a higher death rate because malnutrition, or in exceptional cases famine, would result from reduced food consumption. The rise in mortality would then cause the rate of population growth to decline. Conversely, the cycle could progress as follows: a declining population would lead to lower food prices because of less pressure on consumables, which would increase the purchasing power of real income, resulting in better diets and less mortality. Malthus's preventive check posited the same relationship between population size, food prices and real income, but then argued that a rise in real income led to greater nuptiality, because more people would have the economic means to marry. This would induce a fall in the age of marriage, an increase in marital fertility and hence a rise in population. If one follows the preventive cycle through the opposite course of falling real income then, Malthus argued, rates of marriage would fall, the age of marriage would rise, and there would be fewer childbearing years and thus a lowering of the rate of population growth [66].

MORTALITY

Various hypotheses have been put forward by modern demographic historians to explain the fall in mortality in the century after 1750. How was a saving of four lives per thousand of population achieved during that period? Arguments stressing the role of autonomous influences have been unconvincing. Some historians have noted that the disappearance of plague from England contributed to the decline in death rates. This must surely be a red herring, however, for the last incidence of plague in England was in the 1660s, well before an ascertainable drop in mortality occurred. Explanations pointing to changes in climatic conditions and their effect on micro-organisms can similarly be set aside. Whether or not there was a significant climatic change in England over the course of the early Industrial Revolution, many epidemic diseases are independent of fluctuations in climate and are spread through human contact. It may be that changes occurred over time in the virulence of infectious diseases and in human resistance to infection, but detailed research is still needed to substantiate these hypotheses.

Human influences had a much greater impact on death rates. The nature of their impact, though, is still open to debate. At first sight there appears to be strong evidence to support the view that increased medical provision and hospital care played a significant part in inducing mortality decline. The first voluntary hospital, the Westminster hospital, opened in 1720 and was followed by a further 33 by the end of the eighteenth century. During the same time-period there was a notable rise in the number of dispensaries administering medicine on a free basis to many people, especially in and around the metropolis and in the vicinity of county towns. Dispensaries catered especially for the sick poor, treating them as outpatients with visits from physicians. Along with these developments came an Enlightenment humanitarian interest in physiology, where the medical profession genuinely sought remedies for illness and disease, and philanthropic support for institutions such as public lunatic asylums, lying-in hospitals, orphanages and fever hospitals [63].

Unfortunately, the gains made by increased medical provision were probably not as impressive as these facts suggest. Voluntary hospitals, run by private charity, excluded as a matter of policy those who already had infectious diseases and those claiming poor relief. The latter probably acccounted for possibly a third of the entire population in years of extensive unemployment, bad harvests and high food prices, and yet it was poorer folk who were most susceptible to infectious disease. Patients with terminal illnesses were also usually excluded from voluntary hospitals. Those who were admitted to hospital still faced problems. Major surgery was difficult to carry out: antiseptic and aseptic techniques were not developed until the mid-Victorian period and anaesthetics were unavailable before the 1840s. Surgery was thus painful and dangerous for whatever class of person [63].

The major problem in ascribing to improved medical services a leading role in alleviating mortality was the lack of knowledge of epidemic diseases. Most doctors did not understand the aetiology of diseases in the early Industrial Revolution; they were, in particular, unfamiliar with the germ theory of disease. There were no known solutions to major epidemics of measles, diphtheria, tuberculosis, typhus, cholera and the variety of gastro-enteritic complaints that flourished in dirty conditions and sometimes occurred in epidemic outbreaks. Of these, infantile diarrhoea claimed many lives among babies and young children. When there were major cholera outbreaks in 1831–32 and 1848, public health authorities in local areas were ill-equipped to cope with the problem: sanitation and drainage were often seriously inadequate in polluted urban environments, as Edwin Chadwick found in his survey of Leeds in the early 1840s.

The one killer disease where improvements definitely occurred was smallpox. Inoculation against this disease was common in rural parishes from the 1750s onwards by using matter from infected people. Further advance came when Edward Jenner, a Gloucestershire country doctor, discovered through trial and error a method of injecting cowpox which restricted the development of smallpox in people. Although he did not understand the theory behind his discovery, in effect he had found that antibodies were built up in the bloodstream to produce immunity against smallpox. Jenner and others developed a vaccine against smallpox and this became widely available after 1800. There is no doubt that the battle against smallpox was a major factor – perhaps *the* major factor – in the fight against mortality through disease. As much as 16.5 per cent of the English population had died from smallpox by 1750; smallpox only accounted for 1–2 per cent of all deaths a century later. But it cannot be emphasized too strongly that this was the one killer disease for which an effective cure was available in our period. Improvements in public hygiene and medical care did not affect death rates significantly until the late Victorian period [65]. Moreover, medicine could not reliably save the lives of victims of infectious disease until the discovery of antibiotics in the 1940s. Victorian family doctors knew how to treat some serious ailments through practical experience but they could not 'conquer disease and tame death' [63].

Improvements in personal hygiene, it is sometimes argued, helped to lower death rates during the early Industrial Revolution. Certainly, there was more consumption of soap and wearing of more easily washable cotton clothing. But much of the soap was consumed by industry rather than in homes and one cannot pin down how frequently clothing was washed. The arguments in favour of personal hygiene therefore seem unconvincing. When one thinks of the general pollution that permeated urban life in the early Industrial Revolution, with poor sewage facilities, back-to-back housing, overcrowded living accommodation, proximity to animal waste, and soot and smoke in industrial works, it is difficult to accept that the mortality rate could have been improved by changes in hygiene or the state of the environment [65].

A case has been made for a significant decline in infant mortality in London between the early eighteenth and early nineteenth centuries – based on data from Quaker records – but it is difficult to know whether this stemmed from an improved urban environment with cleaner streets and houses fuelled with coal or whether it resulted from better child-rearing practices [21]. The extent to which the decline in infant mortality occurred elsewhere in the country is unclear, though if proven it could comprise as important an explanation of mortality decline as the spread of inoculation and vaccine to combat smallpox. One should remember, however, that a secular decline in infant mortality in England and Wales did not begin until about 1900.

Apart from smallpox inoculation and vaccine, the other major possible contender for lowering death rates was improved nutrition and diet. Once again, however, the evidence is far from conclusive. Better diet, of course, would build up the ability of lower-income groups to combat infectious disease, and improved nutrition would be especially important for mothers to nurture healthy babies. It has not yet been proven, though, that better nutritional standards were diffused through the English population before the late nineteenth century: this is a subject where data are difficult to gather and to interpret for the entire nation. An increased supply of cows' milk did not lead to better nutrition for mothers because most of them continued to breast-feed and, in any case, pasteurization did not occur until after 1850: much of the cows' milk was thus impure. Not all of the new cereal and leguminous crops associated with improvements in agriculture raised yields per acre, and there is no proof that the lower classes were eating a diet rich in vegetables and fibre. Even if a case can be made for increasing real wages among labourers – which is problematic given variations by region and occupation in an economy where underemployment was common – there was no necessary direct link between better real wages and improved nutrition: much depended on expenditure of income.

FERTILITY

The arguments made for better nutrition as a possible factor in saving lives can also be made for improved fertility: a better diet clearly affects both death and birth rates. Allowing that the case for a better standard of nutrition in stimulating population growth still needs to be proven, what other arguments can be adduced to account for the improvements in fertility that Wrigley and Schofield's findings demonstrate? Illegitimate fertility is the most difficult aspect of improved birth rates to account for. A rise in bastardy rates from 2 to 6 per cent of all births between about 1700 and a century later has not been adequately explained. It was once thought that this might have been caused by a lowering over time of the age of menarche (the time of first menstruation) and that the higher incidence of pre-marital conceptions reflected such a fall. In other words, young women became sexually active at a generally lower age, leading to more conceptions. This is now known not to have been the case because no firm evidence has been supplied about a lowering of the age of menarche [65].

Edward Shorter once hypothesized that the rise in illegitimate fertility reflected a revolution in sexual morality, whereby young girls in cotton mill towns entering the work-force during their teenage years had sufficient freedom from parental constraints, through being independent wage earners, to indulge in sex before marriage [64]. This argument falls flat, however, because studies of the mill towns and their labour force, notably work on the censuses for Preston, has established that most teenage girls earning wages continued to live with their parents [58]. It may be that greater geographical mobility and urbanization during the Industrial Revolution increased the opportunity for sexual liaisons; and it was certainly the case that many girls became pregnant in relationships where there was the expectation of marriage (something that could result, in demographic historians' parlance, in bridal pregnancy). But a really convincing explanation of the rise in illegitimate fertility still awaits its historian.

For the overall rise in the birth rate, the increase in legitimate fertility was much more significant numerically. Here the drop in the age of first marriage for women of about three years between the first half of the eighteenth century and the early nineteenth century is particularly significant when coupled with the greater proportion of married people in the total population. An age of first marriage for women of 23 years, as opposed to 26, meant extra childbearing years were available given that the gap in time between marriage and conception of a child was shorter than it is today and allowing for no change in the rate of conception. A lower age of marriage plus the greater proportion of the population who married helped to increase marital fertility given that the latter was largely the same as natural fertility before the late Victorian period.

The larger number of people marrying seems closely related to the growth of the industrial economy and the proletarianization of the workforce. In early modern times, when most of the population lived on and off the land, it was common for a significant number of people to remain single. Many of them lived in, on farms in extended households, receiving food and lodging as part payment for their work: this was a classic feature of pre-industrial society, of what Peter Laslett memorably dubbed 'the world we have lost' [35]. In this context, most single women presumably practised celibacy given the social constraints on sexual intercourse outside marriage. The growth of a more urbanized, industrial nation led to the emergence of more wages in the economy. Paid work was regularly available in industry and many worked in family groups, with incomes supplemented by the labour of women and children. The growth of wage labour stimulated family consumption. Aided by a consumer revolution in purchasing household goods, the size of the domestic market increased from about £10 million (or £10 per household) in 1700 to £90 million (£40 per household) in 1801 [40, 184].

Some historians consider the growth of family work and incomes to be crucial for understanding how the productivity gains and consumption levels of the early Industrial Revolution were realized [18, 98; 138]. More people married because they had the economic means to do so, and by the second decade of the nineteenth century the largest family size in modern British history was achieved. It is no accident that critics, including Malthus, seized upon the generous allowances of the English parish system of outdoor relief, supplementing unemployed workers' means by dole payments according to bread prices and size of family, as the cushion that supported such large families.

A generation ago most historians writing about English population growth in the early Industrial Revolution tended to pinpoint falling mortality rates as the key variable [e.g. 62]. But we have seen that, apart from the reduction of deaths from smallpox and the possible effects of some medical improvements and nutritional factors, it is now difficult to sustain this view. The research of the Cambridge Group is more compelling in pointing to higher birth rates resulting from greater marital fertility as the key to demographic growth; and an explanation of this increase is closely linked to changing economic conditions – rising real wages over time, higher family incomes, and a greater proportion of the population therefore having the means to marry in a more urbanized, industrial environment. A regional statistic is very telling in this context. In Lancashire by 1800 there was a marked discrepancy in the incidence of nuptiality* in the southern industrialized belt around Liverpool and Manchester and the northern, more agricultural areas around the Fylde and the fringes of the Pennines. In 1800, 40 per cent of those in the age group 17–30 were married in the industrializing areas of Lancashire but only 19 per cent of the same age cohort in rural parts of the county [37].

WAS MALTHUS RIGHT?

How well, it might be asked, do recent research findings fit Malthus's ideas about the growth and decline of populations? Wrigley and Schofield argued that Malthus was correct about the relationship between population growth and food prices up to the time he was writing. Between 1656 and 1731 population and food prices declined but thereafter until 1811 prices increased 2.5 times as the population doubled. It was not until the period 1811–71, after Malthus was writing, that population grew while the price of consumables fell, breaking the traditional link between population growth and price rise [68]. The new situation, as Robert Woods aptly puts it, was that 'population growth could accelerate without economic penalty' [66]. On the relationship between food prices and real income, the Cambridge Group concluded that Malthus correctly recognized that real income would fall if the population grew, but that such a relationship was broken shortly after he wrote his famous essay; at the beginning of the nineteenth century, population rose by an annual rate of 1 per cent and real income grew. Malthus's positive check assumed a direct link between mortality and lack of food. Whether harvest failures and other food shortages caused death frequently is difficult to determine given the lack of data on the cause of death; but though there was sometimes a link, evidence suggests that epidemic diseases, which operated independently of food supplies, were perhaps more significant triggers of mortality. The recent consensus, outlined above, that fertility was closely connected to changes in the age of marriage and the proportion of the population marrying, suggests that Malthus's analysis of how the preventive check operated was perceptive.

SCOTLAND

Demographic data for Scotland, especially those drawn from parish registers, are not as full and reliable as for England, and research into Scottish population history has not achieved the magisterial level of Wrigley and Schofield's research for England. Extrapolating from limited detailed investigations, it appears that Scotland in the period 1750–1800 experienced higher mortality and lower fertility than was the case in England. Crude death rates in Scotland in the 1750s were 31 per thousand compared with 26 per thousand in England. Scotland had more harvest crises than England. It was not until the late eighteenth century that pressure on food resources at such times was relieved by growing commercialization and internal trade, enabling real incomes to increase and food to be bought and transported from more favourable areas. The mean age of marriage for Scottish women appears to have remained at 26 to 27 years in the late eighteenth and early nineteenth centuries, largely because economic conditions were not so favourable as in England. Scotland had a less generous provision of poor relief as well as generally more fluctuations in labourers' wages and less industrial employment. Economic circumstances in Scotland were thus less favourable than in England for greater nuptiality. These hypotheses about Scottish demographic history are tentative, but they suggest that explanations for population development may well diverge north and south of the border [21, 60].

3   AGRICULTURE

Britain's transition from a predominantly rural, pre-industrial nation to a more urbanized, industrialized country was the key change in economic and social development in the century after 1750. Until at least 1811 more people worked either wholly or partly in agriculture, fisheries and forestry than in manufactures, mining and industry, but over the next four decades the roles were reversed. In 1851, 42 per cent of the British labour force (the largest sector) consisted of workers in industry, manufacturing and mining; the next largest category, in agriculture, forestry and fisheries, had fallen to half this share (though, in absolute terms, the number of rural labourers had grown since the early nineteenth century) [23]. Despite the relative decline of workers employed on the land, agricultural production more than doubled between 1750 and 1850. In England and Wales, wheat output increased by 225 per cent, barley by 68 per cent and oats by 65 per cent; the number of cattle brought to Smithfield market rose by 220 per cent; the number of sheep rose by 135 per cent [79]. In Scotland, there were similar gains: oat yields increased between 200 and 300 per cent in the second half of the eighteenth century, and meat output multiplied sixfold between the 1750s and 1820s [55].

These impressive figures enabled agricultural production to exceed the rapidly rising population, avoiding any real sense of a Malthusian crisis. This achievement was not as easy as it seems, however. In the period 1740–90 the rate of growth of agricultural output in England and Wales experienced a decelerating trend and the problem of a burgeoning population outstripping available food resources was not avoided as comfortably as historians once thought [81]. Though there was no famine in Britain after 1700 – a different situation to, say, France, where several famines occurred – there were years of dearth, harvest failure and high food prices, in which rural unrest took place. In the French and Napoleonic war years, there was a run of wet summers and poor harvests, notably in 1795, 1799 and 1812, and grain prices escalated. In some of these years bread rationing was introduced by Royal Proclamation and the use of flour and wheat was severely restricted as a result of the bad harvests. Britain became heavily reliant on grain imports to feed its population during this period.

If the rise of agricultural output was less easily achieved than some accounts suggest, it nevertheless provided a platform for early industrialization; for it is difficult to see how rates of economic growth* could have increased sufficiently in Britain under a system that did not involve better agricultural yields and the shift of population and economy towards more urban, industrial structures. The possible explanations for agricultural productivity* are varied and all are controversial, with little consensus among historians. Partly this is because the timing of the diffusion of changes in British agriculture is difficult to pin down. The highly diverse soils, terrain and agricultural practices found throughout British regions also make generalizations difficult. Aspects of agriculture that need investigation to account for rising output include changes in the structure of agrarian society, looking at the different groups from the great landlords at the top to the rural proletariat at the bottom; the impact of agricultural innovations; the methods by which land and labour productivity were achieved; and the important role of parliamentary enclosure, perhaps the single most significant feature of agricultural reorganization in our period.

AGRARIAN SOCIETY

Agrarian society experienced considerable change during the period from 1750 to 1850. At its apex were the great landowners, protected in handing down their estates by the laws of primogeniture* and strict settlement*; they leased much of their land to tenant farmers. In general the landowners provided the fixed capital* and drew rents from the land, while tenant farmers were responsible for many agricultural improvements discussed below. Yeoman farmers, who could be either owner-occupiers or tenants, also contributed much to the diffusion of new agricultural practices that raised the productivity of the soil [70]. Large landowners engrossed much land into larger estates during the early Industrial Revolution at the expense of owner-occupiers, who were already being squeezed by the mid-eighteenth century. Consolidating land, sometimes through parliamentary enclosure, brought about larger farm sizes, though there was substantial variation in different areas. Thus, for instance, the proportion of open land held in farms of more than 100 acres more than doubled in the south Midlands between the early seventeenth century and 1800, yet in south Lincolnshire there was little alteration in farm size in the period 1770–1850. Small farmers continued to exist in early industrial Britain but their position was gradually eroded. By 1851, 80 per cent of the farmed land in England and Wales consisted of holdings greater than 100 acres (perhaps the minimum acreage to constitute a large farm). One might suppose that large farms were more in the vanguard of improvement than smaller farms, but little evidence is available to substantiate this suggestion. The typical farm of the mid-Victorian period was operated by a tenant farmer under leasehold arrangements, whereby he was under contract to a landlord.

Near the bottom of the agricultural ladder were farm workers, amounting to over a million labourers. They comprised the largest single occupation among male workers by the time of the 1851 census. They included farm servants, day labourers and, increasingly, a landless rural proletariat, all of whom relied entirely on wage labour. There were few remnants of a peasantry in early industrial Britain, a different situation from France where peasants continued to farm the land. Robert Brenner has argued that the disappearance of the peasantry and creation of a rural proletariat in Britain resulted from a joint attack on peasant property by aggrandising landlords and the Crown; in other words, social conflict was the trigger for capitalist production. Landlords squeezed out small farmers and used their power to consolidate farm sizes and create tenancies. Brenner argued that after this happened agricultural output increased as technical change occurred [73]. This is a provocative thesis, but it is open to a number of objections. Two can be mentioned here. Landowners, despite their wealth and social prominence, did not necessarily receive the legal decisions they wanted. Courts often upheld the rights of customary tenants against more powerful sections of agrarian society. Moreover, the availability of mortgages to large landowners seems a more plausible reason why they as a class purchased the freehold or copyhold interests of lesser men rather than because they were in ideological conflict with tenants [21, 89].

Labour productivity in English agriculture probably rose at an annual rate of 0.5 per cent between 1700 and 1850, a more impressive figure than for France [72]. There are no definitive explanations of why this occurred. It may be that fewer labourers had more organized patterns of work and were expected to make more effort than in preindustrial times. The use of more animals on English farms than in the rest of Europe was also significant, helping to raise cereal output through more manuring of the soil and expediting heavy carrying tasks in the countryside. In the early nineteenth century, the replacement at harvest time of the sickle by the scythe (a much larger tool) saved 40 per cent of the labour in harvesting an acre [21]. Dispensing with large numbers of farm servants and substituting day labourers must also have raised labour productivity. It reduced the number of one group of farm workers no longer in demand because of declining living-in arrangements and the dwindling of smaller farms, and replaced them with workers hired and fired ruthlessly according to short-term needs. Whether the increasing gender division of labour on farms also increased productivity during early industrialization, with men dominating high-paid tasks such as harvesting and threshing and women relegated to menial work such as stone-picking and weeding, needs further investigation. At any rate, it was the rural proletariat that provided much of the increase in output because it was concentrated heavily in the grain-growing south-eastern counties of England.

The changing agrarian structure of England and Wales in the eighteenth and nineteenth centuries points to great fluidity but also to a hardening of social relationships connected with the land, with a gulf opening between the great landlords and the rural proletariat. Any real sense of paternalism on the part of the landowners was much reduced during early industrialization; as their estates grew and less regular contact with labourers was needed, they were more likely to look down upon farmhands as underlings. The divisive nature of rural society was even more noticeable in Scotland, partly owing to the lack of a yeoman class there, but also to instability caused by the Highland clearances and the small number of landlords exceeded by a mass of impoverished landless labourers. Scottish landowners had considerable political power and could bolster their security through the law of entail*. They controlled rights over land use that included the power of summary eviction. It is arguable, however, that the provision of poor relief and parish education helped to sweeten the bitter pill of agricultural reorganization for those in the Scottish countryside who did not own land [55].

AGRICULTURAL INNOVATION

Increased agricultural output in the early Industrial Revolution was accompanied by innovation in cereal cultivation, the use of fodder crops and livestock breeding, rather than by the introduction of new machinery. Traditionally, these developments have been linked with the names of prominent 'improvers'. The four-course rotation of crops was attributed largely to the pioneer efforts of Thomas Coke on his home farm at Holkham, Norfolk. The development of the horse-hoe (a wooden plough drawn by horses) and the seed drill were stimulated by the writings of Jethro Tull. Selective livestock breeding was pioneered by Robert Bakewell's experiments in sheep-breeding at his farm at Dishley Grange, Leicestershire. The prominence of turnips among fodder crops was regarded as the legacy of Viscount Townshend ('Turnip Townshend') of Raynham, Norfolk. Each of these 'improvers' deserved his fame, but we now know that more was achieved in the diffusion of these new techniques by tenant farmers and estate stewards than by large landlords. Big landowners poured most of their capital into improving drainage and buildings on farms; and many were absentees and were therefore not directly involved with innovations in farming practice. Tenant farmers, on the other hand, benefited from annually agreed tenant rights from around the turn of the nineteenth century; and this guaranteed them compensation for their improvements when they left farms.

Historians used to argue that changes in farming practice constituted the heart of an 'agricultural revolution' roughly covering the seven decades after 1760, a phenomenon largely coterminous with Britain's early industrialization [e.g. 75]. This is now subject to considerable revision. Examples of supposedly classic eighteenth-century innovations such as the use of turnips for fodder and the spread of market gardening have been cited for areas of the country from dates well before 1700. Indeed, one scholar, Eric Kerridge, has identified many instances of these new practices from the sixteenth and seventeenth centuries and has concluded that an agricultural revolution in fact occurred almost a century before the birth of industrialization [82]. But this thesis is open to doubt because his litany of examples has not established how representative they were as farming practices in the early modern period. Though the timing of agricultural innovations was erratic and their spread throughout different counties followed no determinable trend, it is clear that the diffusion of new techniques occurred mainly in two main phases: in the great age of parliamentary enclosure (the period 1760–1815), and in the subsequent phase of 'high farming' in the decades after the end of the Napoleonic Wars. Changes in agricultural practice were substantial in these two periods, as we shall see, but they were too spread out in time and too patchy in their national impact to be termed an 'agricultural revolution'.

At the heart of the agricultural advance in the eighteenth century lay attempts to improve the extent and fertility of soil under cultivation.

This was done largely by introducing greater rotation of cereal crops and by improving livestock breeding. The need to extract better cereal yields was important in the early Industrial Revolution because of the upsurge in population and the fact that wheaten bread was the staple diet of most people. Under the traditional open-field system of arable farming, crops were rotated but there was always the problem of fallow (i.e. non-productive) land, which was seen as necessary to restore the nitrogen in the soil. This wasteful practice was overcome by the introduction of a four-course rotation of crops that eliminated fallow land and promoted the use of alternating husbandry. The usual method was to rotate wheat, barley, clover and turnips in adjacent fields over a four-year cycle, though variations on this theme were also followed [*Doc. 2*]. Clover and turnips were ideal for animal feed in winter and, in turn, they helped to produce more dung, which fertilized the soil; wheat could thus be sown in fields that had received this nourishment. Pioneered in Norfolk and Suffolk on light soils in the early eighteenth century, this famous technique spread fairly slowly at first in a direction generally from the east to the west of the country. It was used more extensively in the first half of the nineteenth century, again usually on light soils. Yet there were parts of Britain that lacked the terrain or the soil to adopt the technique widely; this is true of most of the Midlands claylands until the introduction of improved drainage in the 1840s, and also of more rugged upland areas such as fells, moors and the Scottish Highlands.

Selective livestock breeding flourished from about the 1740s onwards, but experienced a fairly slow diffusion and uneven national coverage. Bakewell's New Leicester sheep stemmed from experiments at selecting quality animals for inter-breeding, as did the later creation of Southdown sheep. Similar experimentation was carried out for pigs and cattle. In the latter case, Longhorn cattle were created in the late eighteenth century followed by the Shorthorn breed a couple of decades later. Meat yields increased because improved breeding built up the amount of flesh on animals and enabled more carcase to be butchered. Pigs, cattle and sheep had frequently been fattened by farmers, but the new breeds added a better-quality meat supply. Animals bred under improved conditions could usually be slaughtered at younger ages than previously (at two years instead of four). Whether this increase in livestock breeding and its output significantly affected food consumption for the labouring poor remains to be proven, but in theory it should have helped tide over periods of harvest failure (especially in the first half of the nineteenth century when meat prices fell substantially).

Other agricultural improvements occurred in the second half of the eighteenth century. Floating water meadows, giving a thin flow of sediment and water over grass, assisted extra springtime grazing on relatively flat land just as fodder supplies were declining. Marling the ground, which entailed spreading a limy clay on soils, improved the acidity of the soil. Liming brought extra acreage into cultivation and improved soil fertility, especially on heathlands and some downlands. These improved methods of treating the soil were used in some counties well before 1750, but their spread increased in the later eighteenth century. One should also note the influence of a widespread distribution of pamphlets and tracts on agricultural improvement, and the work of the Board of Agriculture in securing a General Enclosure Act in 1801, which aimed to standardize the legal procedures for steering enclosure legislation through Parliament by devolving the work onto local magistrates.

After 1815 a period of 'high farming' ('high' meaning excellent) saw a new phase of improvements in farm practice. By the late 1840s, several new developments had occurred that began to turn agriculture into a manufacturing industry. Soil fertility was improved beyond the gains already achieved by the introduction of superphosphate, chemical fertilizer, and imported bones and guano for manure. Tenant farmers purchased raw materials to process good crops; these included new manures and feeding stuffs such as cotton-seed cake and maize. Inexpensive, machine-made cylindrical pipes proved the answer to drainage problems on poor soils and these, along with the construction of new farm buildings, were capital improvements made by landlords [72, 92]. J. D. Chambers and G. E. Mingay have dubbed the period of 'high farming' one of 'high feeding' because the developments outlined here supplied more meat and dung. The ploughland, enriched by the manure and new raw materials, produced higher yields of grain for sale and of fodder for livestock [75].

Despite these technical advances, little progress was made in deploying agricultural machinery even after iron-made goods became readily available. The seed drill never became popular until the 1840s. Various ploughs were used in some counties by 1800; they included the Rotherham plough which had an iron-plated mould board to turn the soil. As already mentioned, the scythe gradually replaced the sickle as the main tool for separating wheat from straw at harvest-time. Threshing machines were also used by the early nineteenth century. Virtually all other agricultural tasks, however, continued to be undertaken by hand techniques because, with substantial demographic growth and immobility among many rural people, there was plenty of cheap labour available: landowners were not forced into mechanization by labour scarcity. Gradually, the situation changed. Thomas Hardy's novel *Tess of the D'Urbervilles*, set in mid-nineteenth-century Dorset, includes a vivid chapter depicting the intrusion of a threshing machine into a farming community at a time when such machines were a novelty. But it was not until the twentieth century that British agriculture became mechanized to a significant extent; the agricultural innovations outlined in our period were not primarily the result of mechanical solutions.

PARLIAMENTARY ENCLOSURE

Hikers reaching a high point of Offa's Dyke near Knighton can glance down at a geometrical pattern of fields hundreds of feet beneath them and can see at the summit a plaque to King George III ('Farmer George'), who took a keen interest in agricultural improvement. This is an appropriate tribute because the landscape in that part of the Welsh borders includes the recognizable patterns of the hedges and boundaries associated with parliamentary enclosure. About a quarter of the land in England had been enclosed before 1700, but most of this was carried out by private agreement among landowners [96]. The reign of George III, however, was the great age of parliamentary enclosure. Between 1760 and 1800 parliament passed over 1,000 enclosure acts, covering seven million acres, whereas before 1760 only 130 such acts had reached the statute book. Most of this enclosure was clustered in specific agricultural regions, notably in the Midland counties of Oxfordshire, Cambridgeshire, Bedfordshire, Buckinghamshire, Berkshire, Northamptonshire, Leicestershire and Warwickshire. By contrast, little parliamentary enclosure was found in the southwest, the south-east and parts of the north-west [93]. Enclosure could take place when the lord of the manor, the owner of the tithe and four-fifths of the landowners in a parish agreed it could occur and after they had secured parliamentary backing, often with the support of a local landowning MP. This change in the pattern of landholding has always been regarded as a central part of agricultural improvement in the decades when Britain began its industrialization; and the economic causes and consequences of enclosure have attracted vigorous debate, as has the impact of the new system on rural labour.

The chief economic benefit for landlords undertaking parliamentary enclosure was that they had legal title to their land and could improve it as they saw fit without having to take account of the views of the local village community. Instead of the open-field system that stretched back to the days of Chaucer and earlier, in which strips of land were farmed in a common field with few if any lines of demarcation, parliamentary enclosure involved installing hedges and ditches as clear boundaries. By this means, individual property rights were visibly designated as well as being defined by statute law; and the system promoted this capitalist way of landholding over the mutuality and common rights* of the older practice. The costs of enclosure were often considerable because improving landlords constructed new pathways, fences, gates, stiles, stone walls, farmhouses and drainage schemes, to which were added the enclosure commissioners' fees. Even so, enclosed land was worth more than common field land; converting farms from the older to the newer system raised rents by 30 per cent on average [89].

Agricultural innovations could be introduced more easily on enclosed land. Farming one's own property with clearly demarcated boundaries offered the opportunity to operate crop rotations as one wished, to decide what size field fitted individual circumstances; it enabled landowners to keep animals from wandering and reduced the need for a shepherd to drive them to and from a fold; it helped to promote selective breeding and to protect livestock from diseases caught from intermingling with mixed flocks; and it made land reclamation and drainage more feasible [*Doc. 3*]. No longer, as in the open field system, did land have to be either permanent arable or permanent grass. It was much easier to marl or lime soil, or to install floating water meadows, without having to reach communal agreement. Thus parliamentary enclosure enabled farmers to approach cultivation with more flexibility.

In the first important phase of such enclosure, in the 1760s and 1770s, privatization of land led many farmers in the Midlands to convert their operations from cereal cultivation towards livestock rearing. In the next significant phase of enclosing activity, in the 1790s, high food prices stimulated landlords to extend the cultivable area for cereals by reclaiming much waste land on moors and heaths for productive use, and encouraged them to seek better ways of increasing output on soils already tilled. Convertible husbandry was also more adaptable on enclosed farms than under the open-field situation because of the right of owners to exercise their own choice about use of their land.

This is not to suggest that the open fields were necessarily an inefficient or inflexible way of farming. There are examples of improvements made in open-field agriculture in the eighteenth century, notably in Oxfordshire, where clover and sainfoin could be grown in a fallow field as a substitute for grass. A case can also be made for the liberty for cultivators to choose what crops to grow within an open-field arable system, though this only happened in places where individual autonomy in decision-making was feasible. Enclosure did not necessarily provide the impetus for higher grain output. It probably had some impact in stimulating better wheat yields, but these often pre-dated parliamentary enclosure and can be attributed to agricultural innovations irrespective of the field system followed. But it does appear that yields of beans, barley and oats were substantially higher on enclosed farms. Whether enclosed farms increased productivity depended ultimately on the entrepreneurial spirit and practices of their owners, but in general the potential economic benefits to land-owners outlined here appear to have been realized. Although there are instances where open fields competed successfully with enclosed farming, over the long run enclosure produced greater economic benefits.

The social consequences of parliamentary enclosure have long attracted vigorous debate. J. L. and Barbara Hammond in *The Village Labourer* (1912) regarded enclosure as threatening the livelihood of many small farmers, cottagers, squatters and landless labourers, driving them off the land into towns and factories [78]. From Marx to E. P. Thompson, left-wing thinkers and historians have sympathized with this interpretation and have stressed the erosion of common rights and the desperate plight of the rural labourer confronted with enclosure [13, 53]. Whether parliamentary enclosure decreased the amount of labour on the land is, however, difficult to determine. Chambers is perhaps the best-known historian who has challenged this view. Arguing from the fact that the absolute number of agricultural workers increased during the classic decades of parliamentary enclosure, he suggested that more rural labour was required on enclosed farms because of the need for hedging and fencing, improving roads and paths, looking after livestock, and growing corn; and that the social problems caused by underemployment in some parts of rural England resulted from high demographic growth in the late eighteenth and early nineteenth centuries rather than from enclosure *per se*. Chambers accepted that the rural proletariat grew, but he did not regard it as being the result of institutional change [74].

Chambers extrapolated his arguments from a case study of Notting-hamshire. His findings have been challenged by more recent studies of the south and east Midlands that have found no evidence for population growth after enclosure [e.g. 70]. Other points can be made to counteract Chambers's position. The increase in labour productivity referred to above meant that greater agricultural output could be achieved by employing fewer farm workers. Although the absolute numbers of such labourers increased in the first half of the nineteenth century, their relative share of the nation's workforce fell. Thus a release of labour from agriculture to industry did occur and some of it was attributable to enclosure [76]. Where enclosed farms converted from arable to pastoral husbandry, employment declined because fewer workers were needed to tend livestock than to cultivate crops. It is doubtful whether enclosure created long-term employment on farms, because hedging and fencing was only carried out fully once a decade. Furthermore, parliamentary enclosure only affected about a fifth of the agricultural population, and rural poverty was at its worst in unenclosed parishes in southern England. Enclosure provided mainly short-term working opportunities. The resulting seasonal under-employment in agriculture was mitigated by the generous provision of the Old Poor Law, particularly under schemes like the Speenhamland system, originating in 1795, where outdoor relief was linked to a sliding scale that took account of family size and the price of bread. Such generosity in state-aided poor relief was unknown elsewhere in Europe; but it provided fuel for critics of the Poor Laws, notably Malthus who regarded dole payments to the able-bodied as inducing laziness among working people and sanctioning the trend towards larger families.

This is not to suggest that real hardship did not result from enclosure. Although one might question the extent to which cottagers and squatters held common rights in the eighteenth century, the fact that parliamentary enclosure did not deal with use-rights under the common law meant that the ability to graze animals, glean corn, and collect fuel and furze on common land, came under threat. Those who continued to pursue these activities ran the risk of ending up in court. These changing circumstances affected female agricultural work in particular, for women had largely undertaken the fuel-gathering and gleaning. Engrossing of farms through enclosure reduced the independence of many poorer folk in the countryside by enlarging the pool of day labourers; it took away from cottagers 'a valuable stake in the soil' and in some parts of the country saw them crowded into decayed farm houses with no land on which to gain their subsistence [*Doc. 4*].

Most of the dispossessed did not quit the land for the towns; that does appear to be a sentimental myth. Instead, they claimed poor relief when work was slack and endured the cut in their family budget by accepting this form of what we would now call social security. One could regard the operation of poor relief in rural England as supplying a safety valve at a time of changing legal and employment relationships between different classes. But we should not adopt too rosy a picture. Alexander Somerville, in his book *The Whistler at the Plough* (1852), referred to the rural poor's 'oppressive horror' of enclosure. This comment reflected social reality [90]. Agricultural underemployment in the early nineteenth century often involved genuine misery and immobility for the rural poor. From their point of view parliamentary enclosure was regarded as something to be disputed, with delays to work, petitions, and sometimes anti-enclosure riots. Counties where enclosure was prominent, such as Northamptonshire, experienced a wide range of opposition to enclosure [86]. And it is significant that the Captain Swing uprising of 1830, though mainly concerned with threshing machinery, occurred mainly in enclosed parishes in southern England. Enclosure found its poet in John Clare. To him, the fences of the enclosed landscape were constructed 'in little parcels little minds to please/ With men and flocks imprisoned, ill at ease' [89 *p. 159*]. The economic benefits of enclosure aided productivity on the land but the social effects were often seriously damaging to village communities.

4 DOMESTIC INDUSTRY AND PROTO-INDUSTRIALIZATION

Domestic industry flourished throughout Britain in the eighteenth and nineteenth centuries. Before the advent of wage labour in factories, it was characteristic for rural folk to combine seasonal work in agriculture with cottage industry. Dual occupations were common until the mid-eighteenth century because of considerable underemployment in the economy. In the Pennine areas of Yorkshire such a combination of work might involve labour in weavers' cottages during the winter and pastoral farming in the summer. In the west Midlands, high seasonal wages* available in agriculture at harvest-time might be combined with industrial labour at ironworks or in the nailmaking and small metalware trades. Cottage industry also existed in many English towns in the eighteenth century as manufacturing became ever more embedded as part of the urban process. London, Bristol, Birmingham, Manchester, Sheffield, Norwich and other towns were centres of considerable manufacturing activity, with a range of inventiveness and skills, before the urban growth associated with nineteenth-century heavy industry. Smaller urban manufacturing centres also flourished; among them were Wigan, Kidderminster, Coventry, Banbury and Kendal [105]. Spinners, weavers, stockingers and other domestic industrial workers were located in large and small urban centres just as much as in the countryside. These towns had links with the industries of their hinterlands and were centres of much finishing, marketing and production. Eighteenth-century England had more people working in industry, either full- or part-time, than was the case in France. Moreover, the urban and non-agricultural workforce was expanding rapidly: between 1750 and 1800 the rural labour force increased by 18 per cent, but rural non-agricultural workers grew by some 64 per cent and the number of urban workers doubled [21].

The range of domestic industry was considerable in various regions of the country. It included boot-and-shoe making, especially associated with Northamptonshire; nailmaking and the hardware and metalware trades, prominent in Birmingham and the west Midlands; and cutlery, linked with Sheffield. A number of smaller rural cottage industries flourished, mainly connected with female labour. These included lacemaking in Bedfordshire, Buckinghamshire and Northamptonshire (apparently employing 140,000 women in 1780); glovemaking in Oxfordshire, Dorset and the Welsh borders; and strawplaiting in Bedfordshire and Hertfordshire. Very few figures on the output or extent of labour involved in these small-scale industrial processes is available, but much impressionistic material leaves us in no doubt of their widespread nature and regional incidence [99]. It is no accident that Adam Smith's *The Wealth of Nations* (1776) should have taken one such cottage industry, namely pinmaking, to illustrate the division of skills and labour in the industrial world of his time rather than work in large workshops or factories [*Doc. 5*]. The most extensive form of domestic industry, of course, was textiles. Spinning and weaving had flourished for generations in areas such as Devon, Gloucestershire, Norfolk, Suffolk, north-west Wales and the West Riding of Yorkshire. Hosiery manufacture was embedded in the industrial life of Nottinghamshire, Leicestershire and Northamptonshire. And the growth of linens, fustians and cottons in eighteenth-century Lancashire and Scotland also contributed to the domestic textile industry.

These various forms of handicraft work in industry were not just significant before the emergence of factories; they continued to exist throughout the period of Britain's early industrialization. Indeed some cottage industries flourished until the late Victorian period, boot-and-shoe making being a good example. Their existence and scope meant that Britain had a solid platform of industrial work to build upon as she underwent the economic growth and structural change associated with the birth of an industrial nation. Much recent research has tried to link the most prominent type of domestic industry, woollen textiles, and one of its forms of organization, the putting-out system, with the growth of factories through the process known as proto-industrialization. A broad discussion of the nature of work in cottage industry, both within and outside textiles, can provide a basis for weighing the merits and demerits of the theory of proto-industrialization.

WORK IN DOMESTIC INDUSTRY

Work in domestic industry, as its name suggests, was linked to family-based labour in the home and small adjacent or nearby workshops, either in towns, villages or hamlets. In rural areas weaving premises were often long sheds adjacent to farms, a fitting conjuncture given the prevalence of dual occupations in manufacturing and agriculture in the countryside. Husbands, wives, children, sometimes grandparents, helped out with the production of goods. The aim was to provide a sufficient family income to maintain a decent competency and living standard. Given that wage trends for the period about 1780–1820 point to stable or falling wages for adult males, the additional earning power provided by women could make all the difference in maintaining a family budget. In households where cottage industry flourished, women played the leading part in training and organizing the work of children from around the ages of five or six and upwards. For married women, the extra effort required to contribute to the family wage above and beyond the normal round of child-rearing, cooking, cleaning and other household chores meant that their work was literally never done. Indeed, many of the pressures in maintaining homes and work among domestic industrial workers fell upon women who faced little prospect of an independent, personal wage of their own and who, to add insult to injury, were frequently regarded by men as suitable mainly for domestic employment and as subordinate members of male-dominated households [49].

Work in cottage industry was task-orientated, in the sense that it often did not involve strict hours or shifts and continued until specific pieces of work were completed. Irregular and flexible working patterns were the norm; there was no direct imposition of working practices as occurred in factories. Alternating between intense labour and bouts of relaxation, workers in the domestic handicraft trades were largely in control of their own work space and time, though sometimes they had to hire tools. It might be necessary to work very hard to meet deadlines, but then it was common to unwind with a few days of leisure based around games, gambling and drinking that comprised part of a vigorous plebeian culture. In particular, taking off the first day of the working week, a practice known as St Monday, was common, and workers could also choose when to relax and celebrate the holy days of the church calendar. The tradition of St Monday continued to be observed in some industrial regions, notably the west Midlands, until the mid-Victorian era.

The motivation for work amongst the labouring poor in the eighteenth century can either be regarded as lying within a cash nexus of an increasingly commercializing society, where greater intensity and possibly wider social divisions arose out of the demands of a rapidly changing economic environment; or as a continuation of attitudes towards work and leisure that encapsulated a more flexible approach to paid labour and consumption. This reflected a 'moral economy' of life in small towns and the countryside, in which fairness and sensitivity to infringements of long-established customary rights were paramount in determining social behaviour [53]. Whether workers in cottage industry only did sufficient work to tide them over short-term needs for money that they consumed rapidly before exercising a strong leisure preference – an example, if you like, of a pre-capitalist mentality – or whether they were stimulated by the prospect of savings and accumulation and thus were well prepared, when the time came, for factory-based capitalism,* is much debated and probably unprovable one way or the other [37].

Flexible working arrangements should not lead us to conclude that cottage industry was a safe, cosy world, something far preferable by its very nature to factory work; nor should it be assumed that capitalism was absent. Much domestic industrial work was carried out in unclean, noisy, crowded conditions where implements might be stored in the family's living quarters. Tensions could arise in families as the demands for output became due. Fathers, in such situations, could play the role of demanding, grumpy patriarchs. Moreover, wages paid for the product of industrial labour in the home were subject to the decisions of entrepreneurs dealing with a widely available pool of labour. Low pay was common. Though the setting for work was scattered, this was a system based on the rapid turnover of great quantities of goods (though one should hesitate to use the phrase 'mass-produced', in order to avoid the implication that modern factory methods were adopted) [121]. The manufactured products of domestic industry were marketed throughout regions but also dispatched to overseas customers. The scale of their distribution can be discerned by the fact that by 1772 the Yorkshire woollen industry exported 72 per cent of its production and supplied about half of Britain's cloth exports [145].

Most features of domestic work in industry outlined above were found in the putting-out system in textiles. This subcontracting system operated in two ways. In the one, raw material was 'put out' by entrepreneurs to outworkers via agents who travelled around the countryside on horseback, often on packhorse roads; the agents delivered spun yarn to weavers, agreed on a price for the labour, and returned to pick up the woven cloth at a specified date. Merchant-manufacturers controlled raw materials that were supplied to hundreds of workers in cottage industry living over a radius of perhaps fifty miles. The links between entrepreneurs and workers were thus dispersed and indirect. The other method of putting-out placed more emphasis on workers collecting material from urban warehouses maintained by merchant capitalists and returning the finished product there [32, 109]. The putting-out system was characteristic of textile manufacturing in woollens, cottons, silk, hosiery and knitwear, but it was also a feature of brass and copper manufacture, some branches of hardware and some aspects of cutlery production.

In the West Riding of Yorkshire, the organization of domestic woollen production sometimes matched the putting-out system, notably in the worsted weaving areas surrounding Halifax and Bradford where merchant-manufacturers purchased large amounts of wool at fairs and put it out to domestic workers living within twenty or thirty miles. Sometimes, however, woollen production was not so obviously organized along capitalist lines, being under the control of artisan producers. In the area between Leeds and Huddersfield, a great centre of woollen production, master-clothiers owned the wool; they bought it from staplers on credit and employed apprentices and journeymen in the household to assist family members in producing cloth. The finishing processes were carried out under the clothier's own roof until the late eighteenth century, when they were undertaken by machinery in mills. The manufacturer then collected his goods and took them to one of the great marts for woollen cloth, such as the Piece Hall in Halifax, a site built on an impressive scale in 1775, where the material was marketed on stalls [*Doc. 6*]. This is the only surviving cloth hall among similar venues that were prominent in the West Riding in the mid-eighteenth century.

Domestic woollen manufacture involved a complex production network that Defoe wrote about at length in his *Tour through the Whole Island of Great Britain* (1724). It had flourished for a long time before that, but it was central to eighteenth-century textile growth. The different stages of preparing worsteds give us some idea of the complex production cycle followed. Wool was carded into separate fibres, shredded through hand combs, and spun into yarn on a hand wheel. The yarn was made into warp before being put on the loom and then subjected to specialized finishing processes. Workers carrying out these tasks could be part of a wide web of employees. Large outwork firms had substantial amounts of circulating capital and employed more textile workers than was the case in some early factories. In the 1830s the cotton manufacturing firm Dixons of

Carlisle employed 3,500 handloom weavers in the Scottish border area and in Ulster. In the 1840s the hosiery firm of Wards, based at Belper in Derbyshire, provided work for 4,000 knitting frames in the east Midlands. Other examples could be supplied of large enterprises in textile outworking.

THE THEORY OF PROTO-INDUSTRIALIZATION

The theory of proto-industrialization, first put forward by Franklin Mendels in 1972 and linked in particular to the family economy by Hans Medick four years later, attempts to explain how the widespread cottage industries of Europe evolved into modern industrialization [115, 116]. It takes account of previous work on the prevalence of domestic industry before the age of the factory but adds a set of specific linkages encapsulated in a model suggesting how full-scale industrialization began. Proto-industrialization, according to Mendels, takes the region as the proper unit of investigation. It suggests that certain regions in eighteenth-century Europe experienced a growth in rural industry whereby peasant workers supplied cheap labour in agriculture and at the same time supplemented their income with handicraft production in a family context in the home. The usual way this was achieved without sacrificing industrial labour output was for the agricultural work concerned to be mainly pastoral, which was less labour intensive than arable cultivation, or for proto-industrial activity to be located in areas of low agricultural productivity. By these means, rural labourers improved their incomes, were able to marry earlier as a consequence, and boosted population growth by having children who could in time contribute to family income. Women and children helped in various tasks, and these extra working hands helped to combat any falling real wages for male labourers by increasing the family budget. The model therefore implies a considerable supply push with more industrial labour creating greater output without any major change in technology. The markets for the products of proto-industrial activity lay beyond the regions of manufacture, including overseas destinations, and the lure of widespread sales helped to expand rural industry. This emphasis on the commercial dynamism of proto-industrial regions is essential for understanding how such a form of rural industry rose considerably beyond supplying local subsistence needs.

According to the theory, however, there came a point where the growth of proto-industry needed distribution and supervision costs that were sufficient to impel entrepreneurs* to concentrate labour in workshops and factories and install machinery to increase productivity. There was a social reason for the transition from proto-industry to factories because capitalists could impose greater labour discipline in a centralized workplace; to which was added the greater output made possible by new machinery. In this transition into mills, the model suggests that workers in cottage industry often became the backbone of the factory labour force; in other words, proto-industrial activity provided a ready-made source of labour and handicraft skills for the mills. Parallel to these changes, it is argued, came a stimulus to commercial farming to meet the needs of a growing population and industrial labour force: proto-industrial workers had to buy food either because their upland farms had poor soil for crops or because they had insufficient time left after carrying out their industrial tasks to grow their own produce. A region undergoing this sequence of economic change would be one where proto-industrial activity made a successful transition to modern industrialization. Conversely, regions that failed to establish these economic connections would experience de-industrialization, revert to agriculture, and possibly lose people through out-migration.

The appeal of Mendels's formulation is that it provides a model implying specific linkages between different sectors of the economy that impelled regions towards industrialization; it takes account of pastoral agriculture, demographic change, markets and distribution, transfers of labour and capital, and social behaviour. Some historians have argued that the existence of so-called proto-industry in British regions, especially in the Lancashire and Yorkshire textile industries, enabled Britain to begin its industrialization in the late eighteenth century. Others have taken a more sceptical view, believing this is 'a concept too many' which suggests linear connections between different segments of the economy that cannot be verified empirically [32, 104]. The underlying assumption of the theory that factories based on powered machinery were the necessary goal of such changes in industrial organization might also be questioned. How well does the theory stand up in the light of current research? Does it enlighten us about the way in which Britain industrialized? Or is it fuzzy, obfuscatory and best abandoned in favour of a return to the traditional nomenclature of domestic industry?

PROTO-INDUSTRIALIZATION ASSESSED

An evaluation of the theory of proto-industrialization can begin with the problem of timing. Mendels's argument located the growth of proto-industrial communities in the eighteenth century. Domestic industry in textiles, including the putting-out system, had nevertheless existed in England since the Middle Ages and had undergone various periods of expansion and contraction. Indeed, the growth of rural textile production in England in the later medieval period has been linked to manufacturers finding ways of cutting costs in order to sell their product competitively to overseas markets. One might therefore wonder why it was in the eighteenth century that domestic industry should have taken on the characteristics of proto-industry that pushed it towards factory-based industrialization when some crucial features that impelled it to do so were present in times past. The answer to this problem of timing is presumably that it is not really a difficulty given that it was only in the eighteenth century that the particular mix of economic factors – demographic growth, increased commercialization of agriculture, and so on – came together in the ways specified by Mendels and Medick.

This would be fine if the demographic and agricultural links to proto-industry were not somewhat problematic. Whether the existence of proto-industry stimulated population growth through lowering the age of marriage, as the theory suggests, or whether, on the contrary, demographic expansion encouraged proto-industry, is difficult to disentangle; it is a classic chicken-and-egg problem. Detailed local research on Shepshed, a Leicestershire village where the framework knitting industry flourished, has established that a discernible rise in population after 1750 followed the introduction of hosiery manufacture into an agricultural community, and that demographic decline occurred in a neighbouring village, Bottesford, where employment remained linked to the land [112]. But other case studies have yet to appear to indicate the wider application of these findings. There are instances, indeed, where the opposite appears to have occurred; where a labour surplus in a region led to rural impoverishment rather than to a demographically-induced spur to local industry. After all, if low wages and abundant cheap labour were available in a locality as a result of population growth, it might be the case that the move into factories could be delayed. Some doubt must also be cast on the demographic part of the theory because the trend towards greater nuptiality, a lower age of marriage and an increase in marital fertility was a common feature of economic development in the second half of the eighteenth century. Moreover, as chapter 3 has shown, complex changes in the deployment of agricultural workers in the later eighteenth century may have stimulated a greater degree of industrial labour than any specific demographic mechanism.

The phenomenon of deindustrialization was also more complex than the model allowed for. Areas of deindustrialization in Britain between 1750 and 1850 would include Gloucestershire, Devon and East Anglia. In the mid-eighteenth century these all had flourishing textile industries in a largely rural setting, but by about 1850 these had long declined and the areas had lapsed into industrial decay and a return to agricultural work. Study of one regional example, the decline of the East Anglian woollen industry, suggests that the reasons for deindustrialization are difficult to pinpoint. Before 1750 thousands of workers were employed in that region for the production of the New Draperies (i.e. including worsteds); by 1850 East Anglia was largely an agricultural area with a fair amount of rural poverty and low employment prospects. Why did this occur? One broad suggestion has been that regions discovered their own comparative advantage* in either agriculture or industry: over time it was found that cultivating the land with improved techniques was probably more profitable on lighter soils in Norfolk, Suffolk and other parts of southern England than in northern areas where pastoral husbandry prevailed. The problem with this approach, however, is its tendency to explain the outcome of regional comparative advantage rather than the causes of the divergence [103].

Another line of argument is that cheap labour was more plentiful in some regions than in others, and where it was abundant capitalists had the incentive to invest in machinery and factories: it is possible, though not proven conclusively, that the woollen industry of the West Riding had this advantage over the textile goods produced in Norfolk and Suffolk. A third hypothesis is that the East Anglian woollen industry declined, in comparison with Yorkshire woollens, because the latter had better coal supplies to provide steam power in spinning mills, as well as higher-quality cloths and greater export markets [103]. Certainly, by the 1770s there was a change in fashion in sales of worsteds away from the heavy glazed materials produced in Norfolk towards fine merino fabrics with silk decoration from the West Riding. These hypotheses suggest that labour, mineral resources, steam power and overseas markets are important considerations when looking at deindustrialization, but that the causes and chronology of failed regional transitions from proto-industry to industrialization were complex and more varied than Mendels's model suggested.

The transfer of capital and labour into factories by those engaged in proto-industry was also not clearcut; the reality was more variegated. In some cases there was a substantial amount of capital transfer whereby existing outwork firms in Lancashire and Yorkshire textiles and the hosiery trades of the East Midlands did invest in factories and large-scale workshops. A detailed analysis of 150 English cotton mills in 1787 indicated that such a transfer of investment from outwork firms to the factory was undertaken by most entrepreneurs in the industry, but it also pointed out that a quarter of the mill owners at that time had not been previously connected to textiles [164]. Much financial investment in proto-industrial activity by merchants and manufacturers consisted of circulating capital; the same people frequently had fixed capital holdings in other businesses that could not be described as proto-industrial. In Gloucestershire, Wiltshire and East Anglia much capital sunk in proto-industry found its way into agriculture, brewing and retail trading rather than into factories or workshops. It was therefore not a simple matter of extracting funds from putting-out enterprises for investment in factories; the spread of capital was more intricate and fluid than the model implies.

Even less convincing evidence is available about whether the existing handicraft workers in cottage industry provided the main personnel for the labour force in the mills. The issue is not so much whether a proletariat existed before the coming of the factories, for the growth of urban manufacture in the eighteenth century and the divisions of skill that existed were in place before the 1760s [50]. It is rather a question of whether that proletariat became the backbone of workers in the mills, taking the skills and mental outlook with them: on current evidence the jury is out. Arkwright's Cromford mill initially had difficulty attracting unskilled workers because of its remote rural setting; this was solved by securing pauper apprentices, often from far afield. A similar pattern occurred in other factories. In these instances, outworkers did not comprise the bulk of the labour force. Since a great deal of domestic industrial work, notably handloom weaving, remained prominent until the 1830s, it seems doubtful that there was quite the linear progression from cottage-based labour to mill hands that the proto-industrialization model suggests.

Proto-industrialization mainly applies to textile areas. Though aspects of it could be found, as mentioned above, in parts of metal and smallware manufacture, those industries still included much work by artisans who employed apprentices and journeymen throughout the eighteenth century. The metal trades also contained elements of sweated labour, outwork and piecework in their labour organization. Many craft processes carried out in London, including printing, hat-making, engraving and tailoring, were organized via the apprenticeship system, which would lead to journeyman status and eventually the independence of a trained craftsman [21]. Other types of industry such as brickmaking, pottery, papermaking, shoemaking, tanning, corn-milling, soapmaking, glassmaking, iron-smelting, sugar refining, coalmining and shipbuilding were not usually organized along proto-industrial lines. Industrialization occurred in localities that had little proto-industry, notably in ports such as Newcastle upon Tyne, Liverpool and Glasgow; and some areas with extensive cottage industry failed to achieve mechanization and centralization in work organization. Advocates of proto-industrialization would answer these caveats by emphasizing that the textile industries were at the forefront of structural changes in the British economy in the late eighteenth century, and it was in these enterprises that factory production became prominent and formed the basis for Britain's role as workshop of the world in the mid-Victorian era.

Clearly, the debates over proto-industrialization will continue. Current evaluations incline towards a negative assessment of its application to the transition from domestic industry to factory-based work. L. A. Clarkson summarized this view by commenting that the historian 'will find the concept of proto-industrialization more helpful in prompting him to look afresh at the process of industrial development than in providing him with explanations of his findings' [103, *p. 57*]. Industrial organization before the factory age included a variety of complex work structures, of which proto-industrialization was just one. Yet whatever one thinks of the concept, it has helped to refocus research on manufacturing processes outside a factory setting. The significance of domestic industry as a continuing part of Britain's industrializing economy has been re-emphasized. Proto-industrialization also reminds us that the connections between different economic variables that explain the transition from an advanced pre-industrial economy to a modern one are difficult to analyse given the various organizational and regional modes of domestic industry.

5 FACTORY PRODUCTION AND THE TEXTILE INDUSTRIES

The most significant new setting for work in early industrial Britain was the factory (originally 'manufactory', but soon abbreviated for convenience). An early factory, in the form of a silk throwing mill, was constructed on the River Derwent in Derby in 1719 after the Lombe brothers brought back new techniques of manufacturing silk from Italy. But silk was a high-value textile with an inelastic demand*. It was not until the demographic growth and consumer revolution of the second half of the eighteenth century occurred that demand for more readily saleable woollens and cottons began to flourish and textile mills became the premises for the manufacture of a large turnover of goods. Woollens comprised broadcloths, coatings, kerseys, tammies, stuffs, serges and shalloons and a host of other fabrics. Cotton clothing included checks, stripes, plaids, corduroys, plain cottons, lace and fustians (the latter having a linen warp and a cotton weft) [12, 135]. These textiles were suitable for sales in the home market and overseas. Lancashire cotton goods and Yorkshire woollens played a significant role in export growth in the second half of the eighteenth century, as chapter 8 will show.

Woollen cloth had been the leading textile manufactured in England for centuries; in the first three-quarters of the eighteenth century, it was a more valuable export than any other commodity. Cotton, however, was relatively new and barely mentioned in Adam Smith's *The Wealth of Nations;* but it became the quintessential boom industry of early industrial Britain on account of an elastic raw material supply* from overseas, extensive consumer demand for lighter fabrics, and major technical improvements. Estimated output figures reveal the rapid growth of the cotton industry compared with wool. Between 1700 and 1760, the woollen industry grew at an annual rate of 0.97 per cent whereas the much smaller cotton industry had an output of 1.37 per cent per annum. As the production of cotton products escalated, annual output in the industry grew by 6.2 per cent in the 1770s and by 12.76 per cent in the 1780s. Growth after this point was not so spectacular, but the cotton industry still increased its annual output by 6.82 per cent between 1821 and 1831. By contrast, the woollen industry had less impressive figures; in the seventy years after 1760, the greatest period of growth was in the 1820s when annual output rose by 2.03 per cent [20].

The first important factory was Richard Arkwright's cotton mill at Cromford in Derbyshire. Arranged over several floors, this had sufficient space for a complete set of textile machines and lighting by candles for work throughout the night. Powered by large water wheels, Cromford mill opened in 1769 and became the prototype for the new location of textile production. Factories proliferated in the sixty years after 1770: by 1835, for instance, there were 1,113 cotton mills in Britain – 934 in the north of England, 125 in Scotland, and 54 in the English Midlands – and 1,333 woollen and worsted mills. Before 1800 most factories were based on water power but over the next three decades steam power came to dominate their operation. By 1835 steam power was the motive force for three-quarters of the British cotton industry [123].

Originally situated in hilly country areas near good supplies of running water as a power source, mills were later also built in urban environments, especially after steam power began to dominate the industry. Lancashire towns such as Oldham, Blackburn, Bolton and Ashton-under-Lyne grew rapidly in the nineteenth century partly because of the construction of cotton mills and their lure of mass employment. Manchester was so much imbued with the trappings of the industry that it became known as 'cottonopolis'. In the West Riding of Yorkshire, Leeds, Halifax, Bradford and Huddersfield were among the towns where woollen mills came to dominate the urban landscape. They were constructed on a larger scale than most other contemporary buildings not associated with the workings of the government and the Church. Their imposing façades, chimney stacks, smoke, dirt and disciplined work routines aptly qualified them as 'dark satanic mills' in Blake's phrase.

Factory production did not emerge in a vacuum; it was a logical extension of the tools and techniques associated with the domestic textile industries. The impulse to build factories was clearly related to providing greater productivity and profits for entrepreneurs and plenty of space for the installation of machinery. Mills were also an appropriate setting for introducing new working methods based on regulation and supervision that were suitable for handling innovations in equipment. Factory owners could employ workers on one site, making it easier to control labour discipline, and gains could be made in transaction costs* by putting scattered production functions under one roof. Nevertheless, the technology of the woollen and cotton industries developed in such a way that until the 1830s production processes were carried out partly in factories and partly in weavers' cottages. One needs to stress the complementarity of factory and domestic modes of textile production until that time: one could not progress without the other. To concentrate just on what occurred in factories without reference to the continuity from previous textile organization and skills would be to present a distorted view of Britain as an industrializing society.

THE TECHNOLOGY OF SPINNING AND WEAVING

To understand this important theme, one needs to relate technological change to wages and working practices associated with gender roles in the economy. Before 1750, when virtually all textile production took place in small workshops and cottages, often in isolated homesteads, the weaving side of the industry was more advanced technologically than the spinning side. Weaving took place on the handloom, with weavers propelling the shuttle carrying the weft threads through the warp threads. Usually, the work was carried out by men, though there were some female weavers. The introduction of the 'fly shuttle', invented by John Kay of Blackburn in 1733, enabled one weaver to do the work previously carried out by two men because the shuttle now ran on wheels. Spinning, on the other hand, was traditionally a female task (hence the word spinster) and was done on a spinning wheel after the raw fibre had been carded. The great or jersey wheel allowed the worker to spin or to wind on the yarn but not to do both at once; it was therefore a time-consuming process. Since spinning preceded weaving, there were frequently bottlenecks as the quantity of spun yarn proved insufficient for the pace of weavers' work: three or four spinners were required to produce enough material to keep one weaver fully employed.

The situation changed in the second half of the eighteenth century as crucial developments occurred in spinning. The introduction of new machinery speeded up productivity on that side of the industry. James Hargreaves of Oswaldtwistle, Lancashire designed a spinning jenny, a hand-based machine that had several spindles rotating yarn. This invention was in use by the mid-1760s; it enabled workers to spin more than one thread of yarn at a time and could still be used in a domestic setting. A little later it was installed in some factories with a central power supply. The other new textile machines put into productive use were Arkwright's water-frame, first installed at Cromford in the early 1770s, and the spinning mule, invented by Samuel Crompton of Bolton and in operation from the 1780s [*Doc. 7*]. Each owner took out patents to protect their rights to the new equipment. The water-frame, as its name suggests, was the first spinning machine to use water power. A large machine driven by a drum and belt linked to a water wheel, it substituted rollers for spinners' fingers to produce yarn. Crompton's mule soon superseded this machine. A hybrid invention that combined the draughting rollers of the water-frame and the spindle dip-spinning of the jenny, it took considerable skill to operate. Further improvement came in the 1820s with the development of the automatic mule.

Productivity increased apace, as did the quality of yarn produced, with each of these mechanical improvements. Whereas Indian hand spinners of the eighteenth century took more than 50,000 hours to process 100 lb. of cotton, the time taken to produce the same amount of yarn using Crompton's mule was 2,000 hours; this dropped to 135 hours with the use of Roberts's automatic mule in about 1825 [123]. Rapid output was thus a major feature of cotton spinning in Britain's early industrialization. And already by 1812 the costs of capital and labour had fallen dramatically in the cotton industry. The techniques and machines were considerably in advance of those used by Britain's main competitors; hence the rise in the technological transfer of textile methods and machines from Britain to European countries and to the United States in the first half of the nineteenth century [e.g. 134]. In particular, improvements in spinning reinforced advances in calico printing and lacemaking in which Britain had finishing techniques superior to those of its continental competitors by the 1790s.

Cotton spinning machines were installed in factories and worked by skilled male mule spinners. Women were usually excluded from operating the machines: men considered themselves suitable for the work because it offered the highest regular wages in the industry and, it was argued, the machines needed a man's physical strength for their operation – a claim that was only partly true. Thus there was a reversal in gender roles as cotton spinning moved from cottages into factories [130]. A similar situation obtained in the woollen and worsted branch of the hosiery industry in the east Midlands: knitting frames were installed in workshops in the second quarter of the nineteenth century (and worked, as the machines in the cotton mills, by men) whereas the stitching and seaming of garments was carried out by women, often in a domestic setting. Using a knitting frame demanded skill in shaping garments and ensuring an even fabric, and men claimed the status, skills and wages that came with the job [117].

Removed from handling new machinery, women working in textiles joined the large pool of handloom weavers or carried out more menial, unskilled tasks in factories, often in tandem with child labour. Though female employees in cotton mills always outnumbered male workers, as factory reports in the 1830s revealed, they were poorly remunerated for their sweat and toil. In Manchester cotton mills around 1849–51, the highest-paid male job, that of fine cotton spinner, earned between 40 and 45 shillings per week; the lowest paid male work consisted of card room hands, who took home 13 to 15 shillings a week. By contrast, the highest-paid female employment in Manchester cotton mills was as a drawing room tenter, earning a weekly wage of 7 to 11 shillings. Exactly the same story is true of male and female work in other industrial occupations [111]. Women's wages were pegged at a level that was supplementary to family incomes.

Why did weaving lag behind the significant changes in the mechanization of spinning in the early Industrial Revolution? There are two main reasons: a pool of handloom weavers, ever expanding due to rapid demographic growth, could be paid cheap wages because of labour competition; and wool proved to be an intractable fibre for adaptation to power-driven machinery. Power looms were only installed gradually in factories because of this situation. In 1833 the factory inspectors estimated that 100,000 power looms existed in Britain at a time when a quarter of a million handloom weavers still needed work. Sometimes handloom weaving resembled the drudgery of the sweated trades which were part and parcel of industrial life in early Victorian London [101]. By 1850 handloom weaving had more or less collapsed and power looms in factories had taken their place. Mechanization of both sides of the textile industries had become essential to maintain competition and output for markets with our rivals by the mid-Victorian era.

FACTORY WORK

Factory work patterns differed significantly from the domestic industrial setting of craftshops and loomshops. They were based entirely on wage labour rather than on a combination of wages and payment in kind. Regular employment was potentially available, with a weekly wage packet and work for members of a family. Women and children could work together. Pauper apprentices were recruited from parish workhouses as far afield as London to boost the pool of cheap labour at the mills. Work was divided into various gradations of skill and supplemented by many unskilled tasks. It was, as Adam Smith pointed out, work centred on the division of labour – and the division could be based on status, skill, gender, wage levels, and physical space, for employees were scattered over various factory floors [5]. A new time discipline became associated with factories. Rather than the flexible hours of domestic industry and agricultural labour, in which task orientation was significant, factory employment was time-orientated. A regular working week involved the supervision of labour by overseers and clocking in and clocking off, a system pioneered by Josiah Wedgwood in the Potteries. Time was now to be measured by bells, clocks and watches; shifts became the norm; and the pace and intensity of work had to match the working of machines [53, 137].

There were, of course, bleak features of this new working environment. The nature of the work was dirty and often monotonous; long shifts of 12 to 14 hours were typical in the early factories; rules were brought in to regulate labour and operate the plant; very little protection was available to curb the effects of dangerous machinery until the Factory Act of 1844 made some attempt to address the problem; women and children, as suggested above, were exploited as cheap labourers; and fines were given for infringements of regulations. The latter could include swearing and cursing, drunkenness, and poor timekeeping [*Doc. 8*]. In the early factories, fines were levied at rates from 6d to 2 shillings for ordinary offences and from 2 shillings up to a day's wages for more serious misdemeanours [140]. The physical structure of the early factories was offputting to many potential labourers. Mills were often compared to parish Poor Law workhouses or, in the 1790s, referred to as 'Bastilles'. Unskilled labourers disliked the long hours of work and supervision by overseers. Skilled workers in the cotton industry were initially difficult to find because of the premium placed on artisan craft skills in a relatively new and rapidly growing industry.

Despite the model practices of cotton mill owners such as Robert Owen, factories were sometimes run by hard-nosed, tough employers, some of whom favoured corporal punishment for unruly children. In the worst instances, factories were operated by greedy capitalists intent on stressing the divide between employers and employed: their profits, as Marx put it, could be regarded as the unpaid wages of the workers. Female work in the mills was largely confined to young women aged between 15 and 21 years, most of whom were single and who dropped out of the permanent wage force once they married

[49]. Any notion that cotton mill girls were liberated by independent earnings is discounted by the cheap wages paid and the fact that most of them continued to live in the parental home. On top of these factors was insecurity of employment, as labouring hands could be laid off without notice when depression occurred in the industrial economy. Such slumps occurred frequently in cycles, often involving a couple of years in each decade. They could have a serious effect on entire communities: over 60 per cent of the mill workers were unemployed in the Lancashire cotton town of Bolton during the slump of 1842. Once the move had been made into an urban environment based on wage labour, workers could no longer fall back on the traditional mix of dual occupations in agriculture and domestic industry to tide over loss of employment.

To counter these negative attributes, one must remember that factory labour had some positive features. Some leading factory owners, including Arkwright at Cromford and the Gregs at Styal Mill, Cheshire, built factory villages around their works, providing cheap or free artisan housing for their labourers, often supplemented with market gardens, allotments and shops, so that a community life and facilities were available [45]. The Victorian epitome of this extended factory setting was Sir Titus Salt's model industrial village at Saltaire near Bingley in Yorkshire, a community based around the woollen industry. Good work in the factory was frequently rewarded by additional wages, gifts and clothing. Piece work was common in the cotton industry by the early nineteenth century, with employees being rewarded according to their productivity. Owen checked the quality of work done at his New Lanark mill by employing secret monitors who, at the end of every shift, placed a colour on a piece of wood at the end of machines to indicate the quality of the labour. The colours were black, blue, yellow and white, in ascending order, and each person could see how his efforts compared with his workmates'. The best workers received rewards. We might find this method of supervising labour rather quaint, but Owen found that it stimulated industriousness.

Whether or not workers chose or were compelled by economic conditions to search out work in the factories is one of the great unanswered questions of British industrialization, and one virtually impossible to tackle because of inadequate surviving data. Clearly, however, many people considered the lure of regular, weekly, paid employment preferable to eking out a poorly remunerated and precarious living from the land at a time when parliamentary enclosure and the new agricultural practices outlined in chapter 3 affected traditional patterns of rural labour. Regular wages and potential family earnings were an incentive for earlier marriage, especially in industrializing parts of the country (see chapter 2). The consumer revolution of eighteenth-century England percolated downwards even to humble dwellings, providing the impetus for work so that people could spend money on better furnishings and utensils for the home in imitation of the fashionable sectors of society. And because women were a full part of the industrial workforce, they exercised much of the consumer choice in spending for the home. The entrepreneurs of the early Industrial Revolution encouraged factory labour as a means of instilling thrift, sobriety, regular time-keeping, and industriousness amongst a potentially unruly labouring population; but even where they relied on Methodist preachers to spread this utilitarian gospel, they found the links between the Protestant work ethic and the hope of salvation in a better world were a potent spur for many ordinary folk to seek regular paid work [52].

OPPOSITION TO FACTORY WORK

Despite the attractions of factory work in a labouring world where full or partial unemployment was common, there was a substantial, ongoing opposition to new industrial machinery and its associated work practices. This will be discussed in greater detail in the companion to this book, *The Birth of Industrial Britain: Social Change 1750–1850*. An overview of the main forms of resistance and why they found limited support is nevertheless pertinent here. One problem for the industrial worker lay in the poor organization of collective bargaining. Trade unionism in the form of workers' combinations had a long and active history, but it was relatively weak, ineffective, and usually only catered for some labourers with craft skills. The weakness of trade unionism was exposed by the ban imposed on workers' organizations under the Combination Acts; these existed for a quarter of a century (1799–1824) and set down severe penalties for infringement of the legislation. Since there was little parliamentary recognition of workers' grievances, frustration with changing work practices often led to industrial violence. Spinning jennies were destroyed throughout Lancashire in 1769, and there were riots in Blackburn over new textile machinery in 1779. Weavers in west Wiltshire and Gloucestershire frequently protested against the installation of new machinery in mills from the 1770s onwards [141]. In the first decade of the nineteenth century several waves of weavers' strikes occurred in the Midlands, north of England and Scotland, usually after petitions presented to parliament on minimum wage legislation had failed.

The most famous series of protests came with the industrial stop-
pages associated with the Luddites in 1811–12, with some incidents
continuing until 1816. Named after the mythical leader Ned Ludd,
the Luddites were secret groups of workers in the textile districts of
Nottinghamshire, Lancashire and Yorkshire who damaged new
machinery that threatened their livelihoods based on skilled handicraft work [*Doc. 9*]. In Nottinghamshire the Luddite target was the
stocking frames in the hosiery industry; in south Lancashire, it was
the power weaving looms in cotton mills; in Yorkshire, the gig mills
and shearing frames. The government took this industrial threat
seriously, using a network of spies to infiltrate Luddite meetings,
installing 12,000 extra troops in Yorkshire in the summer of 1812 to
deal with the threat to property, and taking suspects to court for trial
and sentencing. Much debate has occurred about the extent of the
political motivation of these protesters. It would not be unfair to
conclude that the Nottinghamshire Luddites were entirely industrial
protesters, whereas evidence of political motivation – planned upris-
ings, hoards of secret weapons, and so on – can be found for some
Yorkshire and Lancashire Luddites [126]. The Luddites never had a
serious chance of causing prolonged serious disturbance, but they
showed that working men in textiles were willing to meet contentious
labour practices with fierce opposition.

Since it was not until after the 1867 Reform Act that most working
men received the franchise, it was difficult to find sufficient parliamentary support to exert pressure on unfair employers via new laws.
Industrial unrest was rife at the end of the Napoleonic Wars, but was
counteracted by a Tory government under Lord Liverpool worried
about the potential threat of unemployment and hardship linked to
the demand for parliamentary reform. Textile districts were prominent in
the Chartist struggles of the 1830s and 1840s, as industrial workers
sought enfranchisement as a means of registering their vulnerable
position in a capitalist economy. But, of course, they failed to achieve
this goal, as none of the six points of the People's Charter, the basis of
the Chartist movement drawn up in 1838, was implemented by parliament at the time. Factory reform legislation was slow, piecemeal,
and originally confined to the health and morals of apprentice labour,
as in the act of 1802 which specified that pauper apprentices were not
to work in mills for more than twelve hours a day. Reductions in
night-time working and the length of the working week were only
achieved by reformers after half a century of intermittent struggle. It
was not until the 1833 Factory Act that there was any official inspec-
tion of factories and not until the 1847 Factory Act that children and

women aged between thirteen and eighteen had a ten hours' maximum working day agreed by statute.

FACTORY LABOUR IN CONTEXT

The arrival of factories was a crucial feature of the organization of production in the textile industries in the century after 1750 and beyond. One must nevertheless be careful, as this and the previous chapter have shown, to place factory labour within the ongoing development of domestic industry. Moreover, by the mid-nineteenth century factories only comprised a significant part of manufacturing in textile regions; most industrial labour continued to be carried out in homes and small workshops until the late Victorian period. The 1851 census revealed that about 5.5 million people were employed in non-mechanized industries whereas about 1.75 million were doing jobs in mechanized industries. It also showed that the collective populations of towns not normally associated with the early Industrial Revolution (Bristol, Plymouth and Hull, for example) and industrial towns without many factories, such as Sheffield and Newcastle upon Tyne, outnumbered well-known factory cities such as Manchester and Leeds. By the mid-nineteenth century, the Birmingham and Black Country area lacked factories and still operated irregular, flexible working hours; nailmaking and boot-and-shoe making took place in a domestic industrial setting; the metalware and hardware trades were housed in modest workshops on the whole [131]. Factories and their organization of labour were obviously important in the birth of industrial Britain but their impact was strictly confined to certain regions by 1850.

6 COAL AND IRON

No discussion of the origins of Britain's industrialization would be complete without considering coal and iron production, for this lay at the heart of major technological developments in the early industrial age. For a small island, Britain had large coal and iron reserves: plentiful, deep seams of carboniferous coal had existed for centuries, and iron ore was also abundant. At the beginning of the eighteenth century, however, coal only had limited domestic and industrial use and there were limitations to the growth of the iron industry. Problems occurred in the supply of coal as a result of difficulties with haulage and drainage, particularly in deeper pits. Domestic consumption of coal was limited because wood was the main source of fuel for a relatively static population living mainly in rural areas. Industrial consumption of coal was hampered by the problem of removing the impurities that existed when it was applied as fuel for iron ore – impurities that caused the iron produced to be brittle and poor in quality [147]. Charcoal was widely used to smelt iron, but it could only be heated in relatively small forges and furnaces scattered around woodland areas.

Over the century after 1750 this situation changed. Rapid population growth and urbanization created more extensive demand* for the domestic use of coal, as urban hearths could hardly be expected to rely entirely on supplies of wood. And in the nineteenth century coal became linked with the rise of gas and electricity. Coal was a source of fuel for the brick and pottery industries, for salt boiling and brewing, and for sugar refining and glassmaking; and some of these industries were also growing after 1750, notably in the Staffordshire pottery towns and the glassmaking areas of south Lancashire. The growth of the iron and steel industries also created more demand for coal as a result of two developments: a major breakthrough in the method of smelting iron with coke, and the use of steam power (both of which are discussed below). By the early nineteenth century a much greater range of iron and steel products was available because of these improvements. Iron was used, as it had been traditionally, for making nails and various types of hardware. It was an essential material for locomotives, rolling stock, iron rails and engineering equipment. Cast iron was used for flywheels, engine beds, beams and cylinders. Steel-cutting tools were needed by craftsmen to make cutlery and razors; and steel edges were a vital part of metal-working tools, scythes, planes and chisels.

New mechanical processes, the design of better tools and the diffusion of mineral fuel technology were crucial to both the coal and iron industries in the early industrial age. Inquisitiveness about new techniques and machinery, of course, spread beyond these two particular industries as the considerable evidence of patenting activity among entrepreneurs seeking returns from the greater centralization, capitalization and mechanization of industry demonstrates [168]. Technological development in the coal, iron and steel industries, though uneven and spread out in time, was important in Britain's economic development. The diffusion of new techniques depended partly on the timing of demand for greater output in metal products and coal, and partly on the acquisition of artisan skills by industrial workers. On the latter point, it seems that considerable ingenuity developed over the course of the eighteenth century by workers learning by doing rather than applying the fruits of formal scientific knowledge; and that engineering skills in particular, such as precision metal working, were highly significant as new techniques able to secure higher productivity [37, 149]. As demonstrated below, the diffusion of new technology often took decades because of the difficulty of securing the interdependency of demand, skills, resources and techniques at a given point in time, but by 1850 much had been achieved in the progress of the iron and coal industries compared with the situation in 1750.

OUTPUT AND REGIONAL DISTRIBUTION

The growth of British coal output was impressive, rising from around 3 million tonnes in 1750 to 30 million tonnes in 1830, a tenfold increase that greatly outpaced population growth in the same period. The surge in coal production continued: by the quinquennium 1850–55, the average annual figure reached 69.5 tonnes [146, 147]. Coal was a regional industry and there was no change in the ten areas of Britain that produced coal in the century after 1750. But there was a shift in the regional distribution of output. The leading coalfield was always in the north-east, straddling the border of Northumberland and Durham; but whereas in 1750 this mining area produced about

40 per cent of total British coal output, by 1850 its share had been reduced to 22 per cent. The major reason for this change lay in the rise of other regional coalfields, notably in south Wales and south Lancashire; growth largely attributable to the emergence of other heavy industries in those areas, with their needs for coal, and the spread of relatively efficient canal links to collieries [151]. Apart from the regions mentioned, coal was also mined in lowland Scotland, Cumberland, the west and east Midlands, Yorkshire, the Forest of Dean, and the Somerset/Gloucestershire fringes of eastern Bristol. The west Midland region had the second largest coalfield in about 1830 and was only overtaken by south Wales in the 1850s. By mid-century, Scotland had an expanding coal industry but was only the fifth largest of the regional coalfields [146, 147].

The iron industry was already growing in the century from 1660 to 1760, the final years of the charcoal iron era. During that period, there was an estimated annual output of 10,000 tons of pig iron which, allowing for loss of metal in the conversion process, would make 7,000 tons of wrought iron per annum. Pig iron output in about 1750 was about 28,000 tons; it had increased eight-fold by 1802 to reach 220,000 tons; it rose further to 500,000 tons by 1825 and two million tons by 1847 [148]. There was a marked shift in the regional location of ironworks during this period of growth. Around 1700 the charcoal iron industry was heavily concentrated in the Forest of Dean and the west Midlands, but there were other ironworks in the Sussex and Kent Wealden areas and in south and north Wales, Cheshire, and north Lancashire. With the use of coke to smelt pig iron into wrought iron, Shropshire's iron industry, originally based around Coalbrookdale, expanded rapidly. By the 1770s Shropshire accounted for 40 per cent of national iron output. The location of the iron industry then shifted notably towards the Celtic fringes of the nation. Between the 1770s and 1815 the south Wales iron industry burgeoned, especially around Merthyr Tydfil where there were some famous works such as Dowlais and Cyfarthfa. By 1815 south Wales produced 35 per cent of English and Welsh iron; Shropshire's share had fallen to 12.5 per cent. Of the other English areas, Staffordshire increased the number of its ironworks and production significantly in this period. Though the famous Carron ironworks had been founded in 1759, Scotland only made 5 per cent of British pig iron output by 1825. After the hot blast was introduced, Scottish output reached almost a quarter of a million tons of iron by 1840 and over half a million tons of pig iron by 1860 [148].

THE TECHNOLOGY OF COALMINING

By about 1750, coal output was restricted partly by lack of technological development. Charcoal was the fuel used for smelting iron in furnaces and it appeared to be available in an elastic supply*, with
relatively low costs to producers. Coal had little industrial use as a
fuel because there had been no general diffusion of techniques of
removing its impurities to smelt iron. There were problems in the
supply of coal, notably the difficulty of sinking pit shafts deeper when
the means of hauling coal to the surface consisted of buckets of water
drawn by ropes and horses circulating around a wooden gin at the pit
head – a time-consuming and wasteful procedure. Flooding underground was another hazard that proved an impediment to coal supply.
Over the century after 1750, as we shall see, some of these difficulties
were overcome. The use of coke to smelt good-quality wrought iron is
discussed below in the section on the technology of the iron industry
but is equally relevant to the upsurge in the industrial demand for
coal. The second momentous improvement in the technology of the
coal industry concerned steam power. This was so important that it
merits a full discussion.

The first steam pumps were developed by Thomas Savery in 1695,
but they were soon superseded by engines designed by Thomas
Newcomen, a Devon engineer. Newcomen steam pumps were
installed in British coalmines from the 1720s onwards. For the first
time in the history of the industry, excess water could be pumped to
the surface and buckets of coal hauled upwards by purely mechanical
means and the use of steam power. Over time this was the means by
which deeper coal seams could be mined. Unfortunately, Newcomen's
steam engines tended to overheat and were rather cumbersome
because of their large beam. Occasionally explosions occurred when
the steam pressure was too great. The solution was to design a more
sophisticated steam engine; and this occurred as demand for new
technology in an expanding economy stimulated engineers to solve
the problem. James Watt, the Scotsman who partnered Matthew
Boulton at the large Soho engineering works in Birmingham, designed
a better steam pump with a rotary engine and a separate condenser
that considerably reduced the steam pressure; this helped to avoid
explosions. Watt's steam engines proved durable and easy to maintain, and were successfully introduced into coalmines from the 1760s
onwards. Watt took out a patent on them in 1769, thus securing to
himself the rights and profits accruing from his ingenuity. A conserva-
tive estimate has shown that, by the 1790s, nearly a thousand Watt
engines were in use in the British coalmining industry [147]. Contem-

poraries highlighted the significance of this development in motive power [e.g. *Doc. 10*].

Nevertheless, the coal industry only underwent a partial technological breakthrough in the century after 1750. Besides the introduction of steam-pumping engines, there were of course other innovations. Increasingly, iron rolley-ways replaced wooden rails underground, thereby helping to improve the haulage of coal from the seam to the bottom of the pit shaft. After 1815 gas safety lamps were available, those designed by Sir Humphry Davy being the most successful. The lamps enabled miners to be protected, to some extent, against the dangerous gases that were part and parcel of coalmining and which accumulated easily in underground passages – choke damp, which caused asphyxiation, and fire damp, a gas which, as its name suggests, ignited easily. The problem of ventilation was tackled by coursing air through the workings by using wooden partitions or brattices (already common by 1830) and later by furnace ventilation (though this method could result in explosions). The use of fans as the best means of ventilating mines was not widely available until the 1860s [146, 147].

In other respects, the technology of coalmining remained the same in 1850 as in 1750. Extracting coal from the face was carried out by various procedures but two main ones predominated. In one, the longwall method, coal was taken from the entire seam; in the other, the pillar-and-stall method, bords and stalls were set up for safety reasons and the coal only extracted from that particular seam. The latter method was more frequently used before 1830 but it was a wasteful way of extracting coal. The longwall method spread rapidly throughout collieries after 1850 as the demand rose for greater productivity and for a larger proportion of the coal to be mined. Gunpowder was used to blast rock and bring down coal before 1830; its obvious dangers were reduced somewhat by the invention of the safety fuse in 1831. Wrought-iron hand implements, mainly picks, wedges and shovels, were used in all methods of coalworking. There was little mechanization to reduce manual labour before the late nineteenth century, though in 1849 the introduction of compressed-air motors held out the possibility of undercutting the coal more efficiently. No solution was really found for the problem of lighting in coalmines before 1850; the traditional method used, lighted candles, remained predominant. This was obviously very hazardous, but naked lights gave much better illumination than safety lamps. Gaslight installations were uncommon in collieries until the 1860s; electric lamps began to supersede them after 1900 [146, 147].

Despite certain aspects of coalmining remaining much the same, the improvements were still significant. By applying steam power to the problems of haulage and drainage, more coal could be extracted efficiently. There was no longer the need to put adits at the side of collieries to remove excess water by force of gravity; and, of course, deeper pit shafts became possible. Most coalmines employed geological experts, known as viewers, to advise on rock strata and where mining could be relatively safe; and techniques of test boring slowly improved to meet the demand. As the coal industry progressed in the nineteenth century, it also gave rise to the gas industry, another important fuel source and one that had not been available before the advent of steam power.

THE TECHNOLOGY OF IRONMAKING AND STEELMAKING

At the beginning of the eighteenth century, the charcoal iron industry was based around furnaces and forges. Pig iron was produced from ore heated at around 1,400 degrees centigrade in a blast furnace. Once the liquefied iron had solidified it was transported to a forge and refined on a charcoal hearth, using bellows to create an air draught. Blast furnaces were usually not clustered together because they needed to get charcoal from local woods. The hearths at the forges depended on water power for the bellows and work hammers. To produce wrought iron, the pig iron was processed at forges. Rolling and slitting mills were also used to flatten the iron bars to make rods for wiredrawers and nailmakers to carry out their work. These processes had been carried on for generations, catering for existing levels of demand. But it is doubtful whether the charcoal iron industry could have expanded to meet the greater industrial uses for iron in the later eighteenth century, because the furnaces needed to be near woods and charcoal moved over a distance of more than five or ten miles crumbled to dust.

The smelting of iron ore was transformed by the discovery in 1709 of a new means of using coal as fuel for producing iron. Attributed to the Quaker ironmaster Abraham Darby, part-proprietor of the Coalbrookdale works, this involved the technique of using coke rather than coal or charcoal as the fuel at furnaces. Darby found that coal's impurities were driven out in the process of heating it into coke (pure carbon) and that the resulting material was purer and more solid; it was passed as molten ore into moulds shaped like pig troughs (hence the phrase pig iron). By the 1770s the Coalbrookdale ironworks was one of the early symbols of an industrializing society, with its multitude of forges and furnaces manned by over 200 workmen. There were varied uses for the cast iron it produced, including the construction over the Severn of the world's first iron bridge [*Doc. 11*]. Darby tried to keep his technical breakthrough a secret, but after decades of use at Coalbrookdale it was copied elsewhere and widely disseminated throughout the industry – another example of the diffusion of technology once the demand was there [150].

The significance of smelting iron with coke cannot be overestimated at a time when there were pressures on charcoal costs and thus the need for successful experimentation with a different fuel source. E. A. Wrigley has characterized the breakthrough as the beginning of a transition from organic to inorganic fuel resources, a shift that occurred in Britain ahead of its European rivals, especially the Low Countries and France. According to this view, charcoal was a fuel that comprised part of an advanced organic economy that was superseded by a mineral-based energy economy centred around coal and metal ores. This protracted process, which differed in its timing in various industries, was the means by which Britain exploited its reserves of mineral fuel effectively and gained increasing returns from widely available energy resources [57].

Further technological improvements to the iron industry followed at regular intervals. In the 1760s the potting and stamping process was developed. Using these methods, silicon was removed from the coke pigs by melting them with coal and the unwanted sulphur from the coal was eradicated by the cold iron being broken into small pieces by heavy stamps, put into covered clay pots, and placed on a coal-fired furnace. The pots were broken once their job was done. Between the 1760s and 1790s, the stamping and potting process converted most pig iron produced into wrought iron. The classic invention for coking pig iron, however, was the puddling and rolling process perfected by Henry Cort in the 1780s. He patented a method of turning iron into bars by passing it while heated through pairs of water-powered rolls, which improved the grain of the iron and squeezed out slag. He took out a second patent for a process that involved stirring (puddling) molten iron by iron bars, which helped to remove carbon. The puddled iron was stirred into a large ball, taken to the forge, hammered and then, as in the first patent, passed while still hot through rolls. Steam power was used for the hammers and rolls. The puddling and rolling process greatly increased the speed and efficiency of producing iron; it eliminated the need for water power because air furnaces were used, and soon became a mainstay of iron production in England and Wales [148].

The first thirty years of the nineteenth century witnessed little new technology in the iron industry. By 1830 the introduction of a wet puddling process in the Black Country speeded up production: calcined furnace slag was used to line puddling hearths, helping to reduce phosphorus and producing a higher yield of wrought iron. But this was superseded in importance by the introduction of the hot blast, patented in 1828 by the Scottish inventor James Neilson. This was a method of heating the air blown into a furnace to increase the combustion temperature. It saved money by reducing fuel consumption, helped remove sulphur, and increased output. It transformed the Scottish iron industry from a position of minor player in the British iron industry to a major participant, and its success led to an expansion of ironworks in the Scottish industrial belt between Glasgow and Edinburgh, notably in Lanarkshire. The adoption of the hot blast spread to south Wales and England after Neilson's patent ran out in 1842.

The great upsurge in British steel production came in the late nineteenth century, but already by about 1750 hand tools made of steel were important for craftsmen. Though statistics are imperfect, steel production in Sheffield, the centre of the industry, reached 40,000 tons in 1853. Steel was traditionally made by the cementation process in a reverberatory furnace in which the fuel and the material were separated, the flame from the burning material passing over the wrought iron by chimney draught. Furnaces produced blister steel (named because of its appearance) which was reheated and beaten by hammers at a forge. The major drawback was that this process produced steel lacking a homogeneous texture. In the 1740s, Benjamin Huntsman of Doncaster achieved a technical breakthrough to solve this problem. He developed a furnace on the outskirts of Sheffield that heated material at very high temperatures in containers made of crucible clay. The product, crucible or cast steel, was more consistent in quality than blistered steel, and it soon became invaluable for use as dies, hammers and high-quality edge tools for dealers in small metal goods. No further technological advances occurred in steelmaking up to the mid-Victorian period [152].

CONSUMPTION AND MARKETS

Very little coal was transported overseas to Europe because of the expensive freight costs for such a high-volume, low-value raw material. Coal exports accounted for only 1.6 per cent of British coal consumption in 1830 and for 6.8 per cent in 1855. A considerable amount of coal from Cumberland was sent to Dublin to serve the Irish domestic market. But most coal mined in Britain was intended for internal use. By the mid-1850s 21 per cent of coal consumption was for domestic hearths, 25 per cent was required for the iron and steel industries, and 30 per cent for other industries [146]. Traditionally, coal from the north-east coalfield, besides serving local needs, was shipped by keelers from staithes on the Tyne, Wear and Tees to collier ships moored at Newcastle and Sunderland and then taken around the East Anglian coast to London, where several inns, especially in Wapping, became well known as destinations for the cargoes. Some of this coal was then dispatched upriver to small market towns, the Thames valley having no nearby coalfield to draw upon. The growth of canals allowed coal to be distributed more widely through internal means of communication; and, as we shall see in chapter 9, coal became the main freight carried on canal barges and their main source of profit.

During the eighteenth century, large quantities of bar iron were imported into Britain, especially from Sweden and Russia, and these need to be added to the domestic pig output to underscore the size of the British iron market. In 1799 British pig iron production was 170,000 tons and bar iron imports gave a pig equivalent of 58,500 tons. But the importance of bar iron imports dropped during the French revolutionary and Napoleonic wars as British costs fell and import tariffs increased. Britain exported considerable quantities of iron-produced goods in the second half of the eighteenth century, especially to transatlantic markets. Iron exports were worth around £700,000 just before the American War of Independence and reached £1 million in 1791. Iron exports dipped towards the end of the French wars but then recovered: between 1830 and 1870 they grew nine times [148]. Although more iron products were exported than coal, the chief market for iron goods was always the industrial sector of the domestic economy, with iron manufacturers concentrating on nails, locks and hinges and ironmasters producing pig, bar and cast iron.

7 ENTREPRENEURS, CAPITAL AND BUSINESS ENTERPRISE

The nature of entrepreneurship, the level of financial resources, and the means of raising capital are central issues in any analysis of early industrial Britain. Entrepreneurs came in various guises. Some aristocratic landowners with control over land and mineral rights diversified their economic activities into other forms of enterprise, thereby boosting their financial status. They included the Curwen, Senhouse and Lowther families of Cumberland, with their interests in shipping and coal mines as well as land, and the Whitbreads of Bedfordshire, who were both landowners and brewers. There were merchants who ventured into manufacturing. Among their number were Anthony Bacon and Richard Crawshay, who had trading interests in London and elsewhere and who provided capital for the famous Cyfarthfa ironworks; the Quaker Champions and Darbys of Bristol who were both merchants and investors at Coalbrookdale; and Benjamin Gott, a successful Leeds woollen merchant who later became a manufacturer on the outskirts of the city. Another group consisted of inventor-entrepreneurs, men such as Richard Arkwright, the owner of Cromford mill and the patentee of the water-frame, and James Watt, inventor of an improved steam engine and partner of Matthew Boulton at the Soho engineering works in Birmingham [24].

The social origins of these entrepreneurs have attracted attention from the days of Samuel Smiles's classic Victorian tract *Self-Help* (1859), with its emphasis on individual thrift, hard work and self-reliance, virtues that enabled the industrialists of eighteenth- and nineteenth-century Britain to rise from rags to riches. Case studies of businessmen have shown this to be a rather simplistic notion, and indeed something unlikely to occur within a generation. In one study of the social mobility of early industrial entrepreneurs – taking Derbyshire leadmining, Nottinghamshire lacemaking and Lancashire cotton spinning as examples – there is evidence that businessmen often took out small shares in different ventures and only achieved success by passing through various stages on a career ladder from apprentice to skilled worker to manager and then partner [164]. But though Smiles's formulation of successful entrepreneurs' origins requires modification, another study found that nearly half of a large sample of businessmen in the early Industrial Revolution did rise from a lower middle class background to become owners of large industrial undertakings [161].

The importance of capital accumulation for the early Industrial Revolution was discussed by Adam Smith in *The Wealth of Nations*, with its emphasis on parsimony and frugality in accruing savings [*Doc. 12*]. Smith argued that increased capital was necessary to support a burgeoning workforce and the productivity of a set number of workers. A similar line of argument was adopted by later political economists. From a different theoretical perspective, Karl Marx's *Das Kapital* (1867) emphasized the importance of the 'primitive' or initial accumulation of capital for industrial growth and the surplus value of labour that was retained by capitalists as their profit. Whether one approaches the significance of capital accumulation and investment from a right-wing or left-wing perspective, regarding entrepreneurial profits as a fair reward for contributing capital to the production process, or as class exploitation of labourers being paid less than the value they create, there is unanimity among economists and historians over the centrality of capital in stimulating industrialization.

Early commentators perceptively realized that funds for investment could be found in many economic sectors and that the amount of money available to entrepreneurs was plentiful: it has long been recognized that the Industrial Revolution in Britain did not suffer from a shortage of savings. Abundant wealth accrued from the marketing of agricultural produce, rents on land, overseas trade and inland transport, investment in government funds and other sources. Much of this was provincial wealth as much as money emanating from the City. Peter Mathias has demonstrated this plenitude in various ways, referring to generally falling or stable interest rates for government borrowing – a sign that capital was readily loanable – and pointing to the sheer amount of money invested in military expenditure in the Napoleonic Wars. The £45 million spent by Britain on its army and navy in one single year of the war, 1809, was a hundred times greater than the fixed capital invested in the entire canal network in that year. Moreover, the cost of the wars against France far outstripped the money pumped into the British canal network in the early Industrial Revolution: total military expenditure between 1793 and 1815 came to £1,000 million, whereas the cost of the entire network of stillwater navigation around 1820 was £20 million [37].

Since the amount of capital available for investment was plentiful, historical attention has focused on the means of raising it. The complex ways in which capital was mobilized and inter-regional financial flows set up explains much about the success of business institutions in the early Industrial Revolution, bearing in mind, naturally, in an expanding era of enterprise, that businessmen misjudging economic fluctuations could find themselves caught in a liquidity crisis that led to bankruptcy. Often business investors spread their capital into different outlets to diversify against risk. Partnerships were much in evidence because they helped to spread risk, though under the Bubble Act of 1720 they were restricted to six people and forbidden from becoming joint-stock concerns, a situation that lasted for just over a century. Limited liability only existed partially in Britain before legislation was passed introducing such protection to investors in the 1850s. Effectively, this meant that manufacturing partners were liable to lose all their assets in a firm if it was declared bankrupt.

It was common to take shares with co-owners in many forms of enterprise. The most elaborate subdivision of shares was in shipowning, which was divided up into portions of halves, quarters, eighths, sixteenths, thirty-seconds and sixty-fourths. In activities supported by parliamentary statutes, notably canal companies, turnpike trusts and railways, the common practice was to offer shares to investors, including rentier interests. But until the issuance of railway stocks in the 1830s and 1840s, no national capital market existed where businessmen could raise loans and buy and sell shares for investment. Mobilizing capital for most industrialists therefore meant either concentrating on fixed capital* or on circulating capital* either from personal and family resources or via the banking network.

FIXED CAPITAL

Capital investment was low in relation to national income in early industrial Britain. Recent estimates suggest that capital investment rose from 8 per cent to 14 per cent of GDP between the 1770s and the early 1790s and that, apart from the decade 1801–10, it stayed at that level until the 1840s [163]. One reason for this low rate of investment lay in the modest fixed capital requirements of many branches of industry. In textiles, for instance, where domestic industry co-existed with factory production at least until the 1830s, the cost of machinery, equipment and workshops was small compared with the need for circulating capital discussed below. Even where mills were constructed, the appearance of heavy fixed costs was deceptive because it was common for the early textile entrepreneurs to build up their premises from small beginnings in a piecemeal fashion. Often the splendid façade of a new factory was the result of an accumulation of buildings constructed after a business had taken time to establish itself. In manufacturing industry outside textiles, heavier fixed capital was sometimes required. This was certainly true of copper, tin and coal mining, where the sinking of deeper pits and the installation of machinery for drainage and haulage was necessary. Generally, however, machinery and factories accounted for less than £1 million of the £9.4 million of gross capital formation in Britain around 1770, and for only £8 million per year out of £40 million in annual average gross capital in the years 1830–35.

The ratio of fixed capital to circulating capital in British industry and commerce rose from parity in about 1750 to 3.3:1 by 1850 [163]. This is not surprising given that the second quarter of the nineteenth century saw a growth in the level of fixed capital requirements for the iron and coal industries, railways, the construction industry and engineering, as the economy became geared to more capital-intensive investment. Before 1820, as we have seen, the relative lack of fixed capital required for many firms was not the result of a shortage of savings in the economy, and existing techniques were often sufficient to sustain industrial development. Jeffrey G. Williamson has argued that competing demands for government loans 'crowded out' investment until about 1825. Britain up to that stage, according to his argument, could not afford to pay for expensive wars and for industrialization: a choice had to be made between the two, and military expenditure claimed the lion's share [175]. This interpretation can nevertheless be challenged. It assumes that full employment was possible, when quite the opposite was the case, and that government borrowing monopolized a single set of resources. Though the case could be supported by the low level of investment in urban housing and utilities before the railway age, it seems more sensible to argue that the fixed capital requirements of the British economy changed over the period of early industrialization, and that in the early decades of that process economic development was not held back by any 'crowding out' of funds from manufacturing industry [21].

THE WEB OF CREDIT

At the heart of business transactions in early industrial Britain lay the web of credit, which permeated the entire economy. The use of credit can be found throughout the textile regions; in pottery towns; in the metalware and hardware districts; in the brewing industry; in agricultural sales; and it was also essential for inland and overseas merchants. Credit linked suppliers of raw materials with middlemen, manufacturers and merchants, often in an elaborate, interlocking chain of debtors and creditors. Its pervasive nature enabled entrepreneurs to keep both their fixed capital investments relatively low and to ward off (at least until the 1820s) some difficulties associated with the lack of cash in the economy. The latter problem stemmed largely from the inefficiency of the Royal Mint, which issued virtually no small copper or silver coins between 1760 and 1820. This led to much counterfeiting of coins using base metals, something that helped to keep the worsted industry of the West Riding of Yorkshire afloat in the 1770s [174]. The lack of legally-struck coins also created problems for industrialists paying their workers in an increasingly wage-based economy; one solution was for entrepreneurs to produce their own coins or trade tokens. This was pioneered in the late 1780s by Thomas Williams of the Anglesey Copper Mines Company and by John Wilkinson, the iron master. The problem was eventually solved with the greater efficiency and improved distribution network of the Mint after 1820 [37].

From time to time, credit crises occurred and businesses collapsed; examples include the financial crisis of 1772, brought on by the failure of the Ayr Bank, and the later crash of 1793, again partly caused by banking imprudence. Both of these financial disasters, and others, sent shock waves through the country [165]. A Scottish ship captain, reflecting on such crashes, noted that the credit-worthiness of even large merchants could 'fall to pieces at once' without them even 'being suspected till the day they shutt up' [189, *p. 114*]. The use of credit also had a contemporary reputation as something that was open to misuse, fraud and deception. Bankruptcies increased sharply after 1770 as the opportunities created by early industrialization led to some injudicious credit transactions, especially among those involved in textiles and trade [166]. Despite these difficulties, it is hard to conceive of business enterprise in eighteenth- and nineteenth-century Britain without the bedrock of widely available credit.

The use of credit has been studied in detail for the Yorkshire woollen industry and for the export trade from British ports to North America in the eighteenth century. In the first instance, staplers bought raw supplies of wool on short credit from farmers and factors and sold it to clothiers on anything up to nine months' credit. Clothiers aimed to buy on a longer credit period than they offered to merchants buying wool at cloth halls; by this means, they could receive payment from purchasers before their own debts with suppliers needed to be settled [32, 108]. A similar system operated in the export trade. The important intermediaries here were large warehousemen, who were often linen-drapers or ironmongers. They acted as wholesalers supplying goods on credit to export merchants and receiving credit from factors who had taken these wares from manufacturers, who in turn were supplied by cottage artisans. Exporters offered credits to their overseas mer-chant customers, who themselves frequently sold them on credit. Thus a chain of credit could stretch from the English provinces to the American backcountry via a series of interested parties. The length of credit offered in the British export trade to North America in the late eighteenth century was usually from six to twelve months. It expanded up to 18 months in times of good trade and was reduced to less than six months when the business cycle experienced a downturn [189, 190]. Fluctuations in credit periods continued into the nine-teenth century. When there was a squeeze on credit available to manu-facturers in the 1830s and 1840s, credit of only two to four months was offered.

The bill of exchange was the chief mechanism through which credit was extended. There were both inland and foreign bills of exchange, the latter always including a specified rate of exchange between different currencies. After 1705 an inland bill worth £20 or more had the same legal status as a foreign bill. Both usually involved the participation of four people in the following manner. A business-man (the drawee) purchased a bill from someone with a supply of them (the drawer) and transmitted the paper note to another businessman (the payee), who submitted it directly to a merchant, bill broker or bank (the payer). If a payer endorsed the bill, he guaranteed to honour the amount written on it within the stated period. Thus a bill payable at 90 days' sight was one that could be cashed after three months. Once the bill had been endorsed it could be transferred from hand to hand as a negotiable instrument. After being cashed, the bill was returned to the original drawer to show that the sum specified had been drawn. The system was something like using a modern cheque except that the financial instrument did not necessarily have to pass through a bank [171]. If the bill was presented to a bank it could be discounted; but it was perfectly legal to circulate bills via the conduit of businessmen without using a bank. The latter practice had the advantage of increasing the money supply. The flexibility offered by bills of exchange was crucial for the credit needs of eighteenth-century business; and the regional flow of bills helped to bind together the financial transactions of the nation before banks existed in many areas. By 1800 specialist bill brokers were common; their income was linked to their skill in discounting bills.

Bills of exchange were only the most prominent of various credit mechanisms. Promissory notes, serving a similar purpose, were mainly used among close-knit circles of businessmen and were not readily assignable. Payment of industrial workers was often carried out by 'truck' or by trade tokens, both of which were forms of credit. Mortgages on land transactions expanded the private credit available in Britain, and became popular from the end of the seventeenth century. They enabled borrowers to convey land to lenders and included a covenant for the return of the land to the mortgagor provided the loan was repaid on time. Mortgages and trusts were held by people throughout the social spectrum, as has been demonstrated in a study of attorneys and the capital market in Lancashire [154]. In these various ways, credit mechanisms permeated the operation of the economy. Credit was an efficient and mobile factor of production* that made use of financial resources which might otherwise have remained dormant. A study of the asset structure of eighteenth-century British firms has shown that credit predominated in large cotton-weaving concerns and substantial breweries and that the share of fixed capital and cash was relatively modest by comparison. The same story is true of business partnerships in some other industries [37, 127].

Whatever the type of credit used, business dealings relied on the trust and obligation inherent in what was often a face-to-face system; businessmen depended on their credit-worthiness and the perception by correspondents and banks that their finances were sound and honourable. Small wonder that some distinct groups of traders, such as Jews, Quakers and Unitarians, preferred to transact business within the strict business code of their own kind. Nonconformist businessmen, as is well known, played a disproportionately large role in relation to their actual numbers in the financing of trade and industry; and though this can be attributed partly to the restriction on their career opportunities by their disqualification for entry into universities or parliament, it also reflected the highly effective, strict codes of conduct that they followed. For a Quaker to be known to be a debtor, for instance, was a matter for public shame; some who fell into this category had to walk in public with their hats covering their faces to avoid accusing glances. It is also not surprising that kinship networks developed throughout industry, agriculture and trade as a safeguard against abusers of credit, with fathers apprenticing sons in their own lines of business, establishing family agency houses in foreign ports and so forth – though, of course, trust in relatives could sometimes go awry.

BANKING

An efflorescence of banking in the eighteenth and early nineteenth centuries greatly aided the provision of credit in the economy. Pride of place should be accorded to the Bank of England, founded in 1694. This institution established public credit on a sound footing and became the bedrock of the 'financial revolution' set on its way in the reign of William III. Its paper instruments became an important circulating medium of exchange and served as promissory notes for short-term credit; they were based on the security of withdrawable deposits. The Bank of England handled the National Debt* and the finances of various government departments. As the conduit through which government borrowing was channelled, it played an important role in financing the frequent wars of the eighteenth century. The Bank of England helped to establish the City as the centre of financial dealings in the metropolis, and its activities were supplemented by the growth nearby of insurance companies, such as the Royal Exchange Assurance and the Sun Fire Office, and by the London Stock Exchange. Together these institutions created firm foundations for business transactions in the metropolis and were an essential provider of stocks, bonds, bills and annuities for businessmen.

During the eighteenth century, private banks also emerged in London in two main locations: Lombard Street, near the Bank of England, and the West End. There were 52 of these banks by 1775, including names that are still part of the banking world today (Barclays, Lloyds, Coutts). In the provinces, banks emerged in the major ports, often with merchant partners, in the quarter-century before the American Revolution, and country banks became the rage in the period 1780–1830. These were local banks, often run by attorneys or industrialists with spare time and cash to invest. The number of country banks escalated from 100 in the early 1780s to around 300 by 1800 and to a peak of 1,100 in 1838 [173]. Merchant banking also emerged in London during the French revolutionary and Napoleonic wars. All English banks other than the Bank of England were denied joint-stock status until legislation passed in 1826, after a severe commercial crisis the year before, authorized other joint-stock banks* outside a 65-mile radius from London. The new joint-stock banks soon began to replace country banks; they offered better accounting procedures, less speculation on capital, and prudent handling of customers [*Doc. 13*].

Government policies indirectly but effectively boosted the importance of banks to the process of industrialization in the French revolutionary and Napeolonic wars. Pitt the Younger gave a fillip to the banking network when he pursued a liberal monetary policy after 1797 in order to secure the support of the Bank of England for the war effort. This policy, which continued until 1819, removed the previous restriction of the money supply by abandoning the gold standard. Whereas the bank had been accustomed to granting credit to the government strictly in relation to its specie reserve, it could now offer credit liberally without any legal penalty. Cheap loans were consequently made available to the government to reduce interest on the National Debt, and the extra taxes imposed on the nation, notably an income tax, assisted with paying for military expenditure. Country and private banks could offer easy credit in the safe knowledge that, as long as the wars continued with France, no significant change in government fiscal policy would occur. The losers in this financial strategy were ordinary consumers, whose living standards were depressed during the course of the war; but the monetary policy pursued, involving the banks, served the dual purpose of coping with military costs and stimulating private investment [172].

Scotland had its own well-developed banking system. Two big public banks were founded in Edinburgh in the early eighteenth century: the Bank of Scotland, and the Royal Bank of Scotland. To these were added a number of flourishing provincial banks, notably in Glasgow; but they were replaced after 1825 by the establishment of the joint-stock Commercial Banking Company of Scotland. The English and Scottish banking systems differed in several respects. Most English banks were restricted by law to a maximum of six partners, whereas north of the border multiple partnerships were permitted. Scotland had more branch networks from an earlier date; the English country banks, by contrast, often operated as single entities without transfer facilities between branches. Until legislation was passed in 1845, Scottish banks could issue notes of smaller denominations than the larger sums required on notes printed by the Bank of England. The Scots, unlike the English and Welsh, also had the legal means to offer a 'running cash' system, whereby entrepreneurs could draw up to a specified sum in the bank's notes [21, 157].

These differences might suggest that the Scottish banking system was more flexible and suitable for the needs of an industrializing economy than the English. But this point should not be pushed too far. Both systems were subject to similar crises of a run on the banks when the economy ran into trouble, as in the financial crises of 1797, when the Bank of England suspended payment in specie, and 1825. Moreover, English and Scottish banks served the same purpose: namely to circulate notes necessary for businessmen to meet short-term credit needs, something which we have already seen was vital to the functioning of the early industrial economy. Banks bought up bills of exchange, made short-term loans, provided notes for overdrafts, and by these means enabled entrepreneurs to use some of their money for investment. There were also many instances of longer-term lending by banks to significant businesses as diverse as the Duke of Bridgewater's canals near Manchester and the Carron iron works [38]. Martin Daunton has judiciously summed up the significance of banks in the early Industrial Revolution: 'By discounting bills, banks were creating currency which was necessary for the growth of the economy; and their provision of "external" credit financed the production, movement, and marketing of goods' [21, *p. 351*]. Altogether, the financial instruments available to British businessmen in the early Industrial Revolution, and the varied means of mobilizing capital on a national basis, were a great boon to entrepreneurs in their drive for profits and business efficiency.

8   FOREIGN TRADE

Britain's foreign trade and shipping increased substantially in the century after 1750. The growing value of trade can be demonstrated briefly by citing statistics for sample years (including re-exports within the export total). In 1752–54 English exports were worth £11,909,000, while the value of imports was £8,203,000. By 1804–06 British exports had risen to reach £51,069,000; imports exceeded this figure, bringing in £55,558,000 worth of materials. By 1854–56 British exports had more than doubled from the figure half a century earlier, being worth £123,506,000; imports were valued at £151,581,000 [180, 181]. The volume of shipping that handled this trade was impressive. In 1786, the first year for which figures are available from the General Register of Shipping, some 1,055,000 tons of merchant shipping were owned at London and the outports. Five-yearly averages for 1820–24 indicate that 2,225,000 tons of foreign-going vessels entered ports in the United Kingdom and 2,073,000 tons cleared out. By 1850–54 the volume had quadrupled; the five-yearly averages were now 8,192,000 tons among entries and 8,542,000 tons among clearances. Coastal shipping was also substantial. In 1841 some 129,091 coastal vessels comprising 10,758,000 tons entered British ports and 140,660 ships with 11,516,000 tons cleared out – a far greater number and volume of ships than those engaged in overseas trade [187].

The growth of British foreign trade in the early Industrial Revolution was accompanied by considerable shifts in its geographical scope and commodity composition. British exports were dominated by textiles, which accounted for at least two-fifths of all manufactured exports in any given year. In 1750 woollens were the leading export commodity, as they had been for centuries, but their dominance was cut back after 1800 by the rise of cotton manufactured goods. In 1784–86 textiles accounted for 46 per cent of British exports: woollens contributed 29 per cent, cottons 6 per cent, and other textiles 11 per cent. In 1844–46 textiles made up 69 per cent of exports: cottons now dominated with 44 per cent followed by woollens (14 per cent) and other textiles (11 per cent). On the import side, most goods consisted of raw cotton imports, other raw materials and non-essential food-stuffs such as tobacco, coffee, sugar and tea. The single most valuable import commodity until the 1820s was West Indian-produced sugar; thereafter it was overtaken by raw cotton brought in largely from the southern United States [180].

The geographical scope of British trade was widespread. Until the 1780s, Europe was the main destination of British exports. The situa-tion shifted in the 1780s and 1790s as merchants in North America and the West Indies boosted their demand for cheap, British manufac-tured goods. Europe regained its leadership in British exports in the first half of the nineteenth century. By 1854–56, 32 per cent of British exports were dispatched to European ports; 28 per cent were sent across the Atlantic; 20 per cent went to Asia; the rest ended up in Latin America, Africa, and Australasia. Imports were mainly from Europe and transatlantic areas. In the mid-1780s most British imports came from Europe, though the United States and the British Caribbean provided a respectable share. By 1854–56, 36 per cent of British imports were from Europe and 29 per cent from North America and the West Indies [180].

These figures provide an essential framework for examining the growing scale of overseas trade, but they also exclude facets of com-merce that were vital components of Britain's maritime strength. For a start, it is important to realize that imports and exports were linked in significant ways. The great growth in exporting cheap cotton goods in the early nineteenth century was made possible by the increasing availability of raw cotton fibre from the United States after Eli Whitney's cotton gin had speeded up the first processing stage of the crop in the 1790s. The dominance of cotton in commodity trade facilitated many a transatlantic shipping passage and helped to sustain an Atlantic economy. It also underpinned the trading strength of the port of Liverpool which, because of its proximity to south Lancashire mills, handled much of the trade in cotton products. Official figures on trade and shipping omit significant areas of commercial activity. Such important generators of wealth as the Atlantic slave trade are not even hinted at in customs records. Sales of enslaved Africans increased sugar production in the British Caribbean and the derived demand from sugar sales in Britain helped to boost exports in the mid-eighteenth century to clothe and house the slaves [193]. Bullion imports were considerable from Spanish America at different times in the eighteenth century, and there was extensive smuggling of tobacco, wine and brandy. A multilateral payments system among ports also boosted merchants' coffers. Merchant dynasties based on intricate family connections plus the growth of ports and their hinterlands were further features of British commercial history stimulated by foreign trade. Moreover, some have argued that an ethos of gentlemanly capitalism underpinned imperial trade and investment, in which southern metropolitan businessmen played a major part [177].

Virtually all this mercantile activity operated under the framework of the Navigation Acts, established in the second half of the seventeenth century, whereby imperial trade was channelled through British ports with British ships and seamen dominating the traffic. Mercantilism lasted longer than is sometimes remembered. Hanoverian governments serviced the National Debt and paid for military expenditure by collecting excises efficiently, enabling the protectionist system to flourish with secure financial support from the state. Free trade*, though much discussed from the time of Adam Smith onwards, only came into being with the repeal of the Corn Laws in 1846 and the dismantling of the Navigation Acts three years later: before then the long-standing protectionist system flourished even though it was sometimes attacked for promoting what some regarded as restrictive tariffs on commerce [*Doc. 14*]. The protection of shipping and trade by the Royal Navy, coupled with the deployment of private privateering vessels, acted as a crucial safeguard for this burgeoning commerce, enabling Britannia to rule the waves during its period of early industrialization. An analysis of the growth of ports, docks and their hinterlands together with consideration of the wealth generated in the Atlantic trades, the growth of export demand and the role of commercial institutions, will demonstrate the vitality and strength of British foreign trade in the early Industrial Revolution.

PORTS AND DOCKS

Many ports were scattered around British shores, but the dominant one was the metropolis. Of 70 ports listed in 1789–91, London accounted for 37 per cent of the shipping entering English ports and for 27 per cent of that clearing them [186]. London was a major port for all sorts of overseas commerce, including traffic with European countries and trade with North America and the West Indies; it also served as a large general entrepôt for commodity distribution and re-export. Until 1813 all British trade to the east and west of the Cape of Good Hope was restricted to the East India Company and ships based in London. The other large surviving joint-stock trading organization, the Hudson's Bay Company, also traded with London. Among other ports there was a great concentration of shipping. In 1785, just nine ports accounted for 86.5 per cent of the foreign-going tonnage belonging to English ports. The major provincial ports pursued wide-ranging commerce. One notable trend in the eighteenth century, however, was the growth of the western ports that accompanied the Atlantic thrust in British overseas trade. By 1783 Bristol specialized increasingly in the Caribbean sugar trade; Liverpool was the slave trading capital of the nation, indeed of the world; and, north of the border, Glasgow was an important entrepôt for the Chesapeake tobacco trade [183, 185, 189]. Many other ports tended to specialize in their activities. North-eastern ports such as Newcastle, Sunderland and Whitby were prominent in the coal trade; Hull had a substantial trade with the Baltic and northern Europe; Great Yarmouth and Lowestoft were fishing ports; and Chatham, Portsmouth and Plymouth were thriving dockyard towns with sizeable workforces and burgeoning activity during wartime.

The vigorous growth of many ports was accompanied by the building of wet docks. The pioneer in such developments was Liverpool, where six docks were built in the eighteenth century [*Doc. 15*]. A further five were added between 1811 and 1836, some being steamship docks. This building programme, much of it supported by the local corporation, meant that two-and-half miles of the Mersey had docks by the mid-nineteenth century [185]. Elsewhere, docks were constructed more slowly. At Bristol the problem of shipping congestion on the River Avon was not helped by parsimonious local interests that gave rather lukewarm support to dock construction. The building of the Floating Harbour (1804–09) only partially removed Bristol's port congestion; the problem was not resolved until the port was removed downriver to Avonmouth in the 1870s. At Glasgow, the navigation of the Clyde was deepened and improved in the early nineteenth century and an East India harbour constructed at Greenock in 1809. In London there was much overcrowding on the Thames for most of the eighteenth century, caused by the sheer number and size of ships using the metropolis and by the requirement that vessels had to load and unload at the legal quays. Though the port of London was handicapped by the lack of a single dock authority, an efflorescence in dock construction led to the opening of the West India Dock (1803), East India Dock (1806) and St Katherine's Dock (1825) among others, which meant that by 1830 London had approximately 70 acres of docks costing over £7 million [186, 187].

Better docks enabled larger ships to berth on estuarine rivers; they protected vessels against damage and allowed for more efficient loading and unloading of cargoes. They often had large warehouses built on their sites. Providing work for packers, hauliers, shipwrights, sailors, customs officers and many other people, they were hives of bustling activity. Ports with dockyards soon proved their utility to local business, but how important were docks to the process of economic development? No historian would argue that they were essential for trade growth, because ports had often flourished with rather inadequate facilities. Yet docks were crucial for handling the increased volume of coastal and foreign shipping flowing in and out of British harbours during the Industrial Revolution, and they made a major difference to the performance of leading ports. As Gordon Jackson has written, without the expansion of port and dock facilities 'it is difficult to envisage how the industrial heartland of England could have developed as it did' [186, *p. 206*]. Improved ports and docks made their greatest impact in cities where there was a flourishing hinterland with manufacturing, demographic growth and improved internal communications, such as Liverpool after about 1770, or where the functions of a leading industrial centre were combined with shipping facilities in one urban space, as in Glasgow by about 1830 [183, 188].

THE WEALTH OF THE EMPIRE

For the eighteenth century, possible connections between the wealth generated in the empire and the onset of British industrialization were first given wide currency in Eric Williams's *Capitalism and Slavery* (1944). Williams showed that, by the late eighteenth century, Liverpool was booming on the back of the slave trade at the same time that industrialization, notably factory-based cotton-spinning, was becoming firmly established in south Lancashire. He considered that there must surely be an economic link between these two phenomena, and that the connection lay in channelling the profits from slavery and the slave trade into industry. The scale of the traffic in enslaved Africans was enormous. English vessels shipped some 2.7 million slaves across the Atlantic during the eighteenth century. In 1776 the valuation of sugar estates in Jamaica alone (based, of course, on slave labour) amounted to £18 million sterling (about £9 billion in today's money), which accounted for half of British investment in the Caribbean. Williams argued that the profits obtained from the triangular trade and slavery provided one of the main streams of capital accumulation that financed the Industrial Revolution in Britain [194].

Since he wrote those words, modern research has cast doubt on this view. The risks of the slave trade meant that annual net returns in the trade averaged less than 10 per cent on capital outlay in the period 1740–1807. Slave-trade profits amounted to over 0.5 per cent of British national income* in only one period between 1688 and 1800. Moreover, despite the wealth created by sugar and slaves, the contribution of plantation profits to industrial investment was not clear-cut. Some families transferred funds from their Jamaican sugar estates to domestic industrial enterprise; among them were the Pennants, who invested in slate quarries in north Wales, and the Fullers, who owned ironworks and gun foundries in Sussex. But other families that accrued substantial West Indian fortunes, notably the Pinneys and the Beckfords, invested in government funds and land in England but did not put much of their wealth into domestic industry. In fact, for absentee proprietors it was probably difficult to extract their money from the Caribbean because so much of it was tied up in plantation and mortgage debts [190].

It is equally difficult to prove that merchant capital amassed from colonial commerce was decisive for industrial investment in Britain. Profits earned in the Atlantic trades were undoubtedly put into ship-building, snuff mills, sugar refineries, glassworks, ironworks, textiles, leather manufactories, coalmines and other industrial enterprises in the major British ports and their hinterlands. But from surviving records it is impossible to establish what proportion of merchants' investment in industry originated from overseas trade rather than from sources such as banking, insurance, land and government stock. The case of Glasgow is instructive: no substantial transfer of capital from the tobacco trade to the Scottish cotton industry occurred because by around 1795 only about 17 per cent of the value of cotton firms north of the border was financed by colonial traders. On a much broader level, the extent to which wealth generated in the colonies became an important source of capital accumulation in metropolitan Britain has been questioned. Careful estimates show that commerce with the wider world generated funds sufficient to finance only 15 per cent of gross investment expenditures during the Industrial Revolution [190].

EXPORTS AND ECONOMIC GROWTH

To determine whether exports acted as a trigger for economic growth, one needs data on the proportion of industrial output that was exported. This is problematic because we lack accurate production estimates for many branches of British industry. It seems, however, that the proportion of industrial output exported rose from about one-fifth in 1700 to about one-third in 1800 and then fell back to around one-quarter by 1851. But there was considerable variation among individual industries. Exports of copper and brass – both comparatively small industries in the eighteenth century – accounted for about 40 per cent of production on the eve of the American Revolution, while the nailmaking trades were said to export three-quarters of their output to British America by the 1760s. Two branches of textiles were very reliant on exports. The woollen industry sold 45 per cent of its product abroad in 1772, 55 per cent in 1799, but only 19 per cent in 1831. The most significant industry with a high ratio of exports to production was cotton, which sold 50 per cent of its manufacture abroad in 1760, 62 per cent in 1801 and 56 per cent in 1831 [20, 190].

What do these percentages suggest about the relationship between exports and economic growth? Historians who see the home market as the mainspring of economic growth in eighteenth-century Britain might argue that only one industry (cotton) ever had more than half of its product exported – and then only in certain years in the period 1760–1801. A good case could be made, in fact, for cotton being the one British industry that was essentially nourished by overseas trade. Estimates of sectoral growth rates in eighteenth-century British industry show a steady rise in the output of various industries, including many that did not provide significant exports (soap, coal, brewing, building and construction are examples) [20]. This broadly-based industrial output for the domestic market underscores the significance of home demand for economic growth. Some commentators link this domestic demand to the percolation of the 'consumer revolution' throughout the home market in the eighteenth century, with all groups except the indigent poor spending savings on furniture, glassware, domestic utensils, textile clothing, sugar consumption, and fashionable beverages such as tea and coffee [40].

A strong case can nevertheless be made for exports as a generator of growth in the late eighteenth century. The increase in the quantity and variety of manufactured exports encouraged the development of the non-agricultural sector of the British economy, and diversified foreign trade so that it was no longer import-led. British merchants sold goods to American markets at a critical period in the mid-eighteenth century when long-standing European markets for woollens and worsteds were in decline and when exports, rather than agricultural incomes, were becoming a major stimulus to manufacturing [88]. Without markets in the colonies, British industries would not have had so much incentive for rapid expansion at that time. The large trading bowl of Britain's overseas trade became vital after 1750 for industrializing areas because it gave added incentive for manufacturers to quicken the productivity of textiles, metalware and hardware through extra employment, the division of labour, and improved commercial organization: in this way supply* and demand* intermeshed.

If the labour force had produced mainly for the home market without the stimulus of expanding exports, lower levels of productivity would have been achieved because of prevailing unemployment, underemployment and cheap labour. After 1770 the rapid growth of cotton exports may have stimulated technological improvements on the spinning side of the industry by creating a larger market for finished cotton goods. Certainly, the diffusion of the technological breakthrough accelerated during the export boom of the last twenty years of the century. By 1800, British industrial output was not circumscribed by home demand, and the domestic market had also probably increased partly through productivity induced by overseas trade. Integration of the export sector into an economy with increased manufacturing may well have been crucial in giving Britain a comparative advantage over other regions of western Europe poised for industrialization in the late eighteenth century [190].

British exports contributed between 7 and 11 per cent of national income at various points between 1770 and 1841; they only accounted for a 12 per cent share by the 1840s. By that time, Britain was dispatching a much higher proportion of its industrial output abroad than either France or Germany. But Britain's economic strength depended on a limited range of export industries, with textiles and iron predominating: the greater diversification of exports characteristic of the quarter-century before the American Revolution had been pegged back. As the terms of trade moved against Britain in the first half of the nineteenth century, production costs and export prices dropped in cotton textiles but exports of cheap cotton clothing continued at an even faster pace than before. Both for the cotton industry and exports generally, it seems that the much greater volume of manufactured wares sent abroad in the period 1800–60 was stimulated more by increased efficiency in the supply of goods than by an expansive foreign demand.

COMMERCIAL INSTITUTIONS

There were important links between overseas trade and business development in the British economy. Merchants participated in an uncertain trading world where commercial communication was based on letters and was thus subject to considerable delay and inconvenience. High risks from uncertain price changes, frequent wars, and a tendency to overspeculate, could create volatile trading conditions. It is therefore no surprise that bankrupt merchants became a recognizable feature of the British economy. Potential difficulties were mitigated, however, by the increased sophistication in the finance of commerce that accompanied the growing scale and intricacy of foreign trade. An international payments mechanism involving bills of exchange enabled transfers to be made on either a bilateral or multilateral basis between Britain and overseas ports. Marine insurance also benefited from the growth of oceanic commerce; indeed, the two were mutually reinforcing. The livelihood of underwriters at the London Assurance Company, the Royal Exchange Assurance and Lloyd's Coffee House – the three early centres of British marine insurance – was closely linked to the higher premiums charged for hazardous long-distance voyages during eighteenth-century wars.

The growth of Atlantic trade in particular helped to foster the development of banking at the outports. Between 1750 and 1775, colonial merchants became prominent partners in the first banks established in Bristol, Glasgow and Liverpool, for the availability of deposit and transfer facilities suited the needs of substantial businessmen. The provision of credit was a further way in which international trade was connected with more efficient financial transactions. Most export goods were bought and sold on nine to twelve months' credit before payment was required, which was usually more generous than foreign firms offered when, after 1783, the United States could trade outside British mercantile control. The chain of credit linking suppliers of goods in provincial Britain, merchants at various ports, and overseas customers, affected many commercial decisions in foreign trade, and offered flexible payment for goods [192]. Merchants' correspondence specified credit terms and supplied details of interest charges, discounts, and procedures in handling bills of exchange [*Doc. 16*]. The slave trade played a significant role in the deployment of credit over long distances, for this most risky of all eighteenth-century trades could not have functioned without the long credits offered to suppliers of trade goods for Africa and to American purchasers of enslaved Africans.

During the eighteenth century, merchant firms in several major trades became more concentrated in number, giving advantages of scale in the handling of a wide range of goods; this occurred particularly in the tobacco, sugar and slave trades. Along with this rise in concentration ratios came the growth of substantial wholesalers in leading ports, men such as ironmongers, drapers and warehousemen, who acquired goods for credit and sold them on longer credit. British merchants also adapted their roles to changing economic circumstances. In the last quarter of the eighteenth century, manufacturers in northern areas extended their role into overseas marketing and some merchants became manufacturers as well. A new generation of specialists replaced them towards the end of the French wars after some of the long-established merchant houses had retired or gone bankrupt. These were often commission agents resident abroad, usually with a partner in Britain, or pure manufacturers, providing credits for exporters to send their goods overseas. These merchants were called 'accepting houses' (i.e. they accepted bills of exchange). Some later became merchant bankers, including famous firms such as Barings and Rothschilds. Another business development in the first half of the nineteenth century was the emergence of 'agency houses', often buying and selling on commission, and operating especially in the markets of India and south-east Asia [178].

The significance of these developments in mercantile business was that British traders, demonstrating their adaptability and resilience in changing circumstances, helped to develop an important framework of business institutions for the economy that served it well in the long run. The commercial and financial institutions discussed here, together with the development of commercial practices and law, left 'an infrastructure of great utility to the entire economy in the ensuing era of rapid industrialization and attendant export growth' [192, *p. 283*]. In a nutshell, the economic changes through which Britain progressed in the century after 1750 were as much an entrepreneurial revolution as an Industrial Revolution; and those historians who question the extent of the quantitative input of British foreign trade to economic growth should not ignore the contribution of these significant business changes to the performance of the economy.

9   INTERNAL TRANSPORT

An improved system of transport was a necessary part of Britain's early industrialization. Only by this means could the raw materials and industrial products of different regions be moved over distances from their point of production to their place of consumption. Traditionally, most goods had been transported either on the roads or via river navigations. Waggons and carts transferred agricultural samples, gold, silver and copper, industrial goods, and, to a limited extent, were also involved in passenger travel. River boats and barges concentrated on the haulage of heavy raw materials such as gravel, slate, brick and timber, but also carried barley, malt, corn and other agricultural commodities; their most important freight, however, was coal. These modes of transport continued to exist in 1850 as they had done in 1750 but were improved by newer developments such as canals and railways, both of which necessitated substantial financial investment. There were also important changes in the costs of internal transport in the century after 1750 and, on the roads and railways, in the speed of travel. Whether the different types of transport effectively complemented one another and provided a truly nationwide network of internal communications will be discussed later.

THE DEVELOPMENT OF WATERWAYS

The main navigable rivers in England were the Thames, the Severn, the Yorkshire Ouse, the Humber, the Trent, and the Mersey. Improvements to the navigation of these riverine routes had been made in the first half of the eighteenth century, often as a result of parliamentary legislation. Generally, the rivers had some of their meanders straightened, weirs mended, towpaths constructed, and banks strengthened. These may seem rather humdrum improvements. Nevertheless, they increased the distance over which goods could be marketed effectively, especially into interior parts of the country ill served by waterways. Thus already by 1750, for instance, the Severn was navigable as far north as Welshpool and Thames barges could reach Lechlade. The slow nature of economic growth in the early eighteenth century meant that water transport could be contained satisfactorily by an extension of the existing river networks. Yet by 1750 it was clear that further improvements would be needed to cope with the greater industrial and agricultural output that served the needs of a rapidly growing population.

In the second half of the eighteenth century, additional parliamentary legislation helped to improve the river navigations. This was particularly the case with the Thames where the Thames Navigation Commission was responsible for improving locks, weirs and mills. Perhaps the greatest improvement was the gradual replacement of existing single or 'flash' locks at weirs with double or 'pound' locks. Flash locks were wooden structures, consisting of horizontal and vertical slats. Lock-keepers removed the vertical slats once a head of water had built up, to enable boats and barges to come over locks on the flash. The problem, of course, was that the wood often shattered and it proved difficult to regulate the flow of water. Accidents occurred; and the system of flash locks was cumbersome, making water traffic relatively slow. The introduction of the pound lock solved the problem by enabling the water to be equalized on either side of the lock and by providing a more durable structure. Pound locks were not a new invention; they had been used on Dutch waterways since the sixteenth century. But they were only installed on English waterways after 1760 when the economic demands for improved transport provided the impetus. Other engineering achievements on the canals included cutting and embanking, erection of tunnels, bridges and aqueducts, and a large number of waggonways linked to canals built by labourers or 'navigators' (hence 'navvies') [200].

At the heart of new developments in internal transport in our period lay the growth of canals. The Sankey Brook navigation, a short canalized stream leading from St Helens to the Mersey near Bootle, is sometimes regarded as the first English canal. This particular navigation was altered in 1757. But the canal age really started with the Duke of Bridgewater's canal, opened in 1761, which stretched from the duke's coalpits at Worsley into the centre of Manchester, a distance of about eight miles. This canal was distinctive in that it had a splendid aqueduct and an underwater passage on which people took pleasure trips – features that were much admired by contemporaries [12]. Yet the duke's canal also incorporated the main characteristics of this new form of transport: artificially created still water; pound locks; a route specially designed to link industry with the hub of a growing urban centre; and, not least, coal as the main freight. The Duke of Bridgewater, in a famous phrase, said that a successful canal would have 'coals at the heel of it'; and indeed coal was the chief commodity carried on waterways, particularly in south Wales, the Midlands and the north of England. Canals enabled coal from inland coal seams to reach wider regional markets: in the Black Country alone perhaps as much as two million tons of coal was being transported on the canals surrounding Birmingham by the mid-1840s [213].

The building of canals soon spread. They comprised the bulk of the 52 parliamentary acts for inland navigation passed between 1759 and 1774, and were mainly concentrated in the Midlands and north of England. In the 1760s and 1770s the new waterways tended to be smaller, narrowboat canals with an average lock width of 7 feet; thereafter, trunk canals some 14 feet in width were also constructed, such as the Leeds and Liverpool, Forth and Clyde, Thames and Severn, and Kennet and Avon canals, though these often took years to complete. There was a particular spate of canal building in the period 1790–94, a canal mania, in which 82 navigation acts, including 51 new projects, were sanctioned by parliament. During the French revolutionary and Napoleonic wars, canal building slowed up – the easy access to credit of the 1780s had dried up and inflation* became a problem for investors. But even in this period there were notable developments, such as the construction of the Grand Junction canal between 1793 and 1805, the main waterway between London and the industrial west Midlands. By about 1820 the extension of waterborne communications meant that there were about 2,000 miles of river navigation open for traffic and about the same mileage for canals in England and Wales (as opposed to about 1,400 miles of navigable waterways, nearly all rivers, in 1760). The main triggers for the fluctuating spurts in the construction of canals were the economic demands of particular localities, periods of trade growth, and evidence of the profitability of existing canals [200].

Already by 1790 the growth of the early canal network and its links with existing river navigations meant that, in theory, two west-coast ports, Bristol and Liverpool, and two east-coast ports, London and Hull, were linked entirely by waterborne means of communication [38]. Canals were constructed particularly in and around Birmingham (for instance, the Staffordshire canal) and in south Lancashire. By 1800 Liverpool was a port whose hinterland was criss-crossed with canals [188]. Important existing river systems had canals attached to them. The Thames was connected to the Kennet and Avon canal, the Coventry canal and the Oxford canal, enabling waterborne transport to spread out in a westerly and a northerly direction. By the turn of the nineteenth century, the Severn was linked up to no less than fourteen canals. Southern agricultural England and London, with the exception of the Grand Junction canal, were less well served by canals but then there was generally less need for them in that region.

Carriage services on the waterways were usually the preserve of small independent carriers operating barges either with a crew of 'bow halers' to haul the boats or with a team of horses; the latter method was usually cheaper and more efficient [*Doc. 17*]. But there were some larger common carriers, such as Pickford's, which owned 116 canal barges by 1838 and operated throughout a large section of England. By 1830 some canal companies had attempted to speed up transit time by introducing fly-boat services, but in general canal traffic was a relatively slow form of communication. Nevertheless, canals were an important feature of an industrializing society because they linked up inland centres of industry with ports and provided essential raw materials and fuel to a rapidly urbanizing population [*Doc. 18*]. They were also significant in rural parts of England in facilitating trade in agricultural products. By the early nineteenth century, once a substantial network of waterways was in place, waterborne traffic across regions was crucial for the interchange of agricultural and industrial commodities. Water transport was also relatively cheap compared with road traffic, because more horses and waggons were needed to haul goods than were necessary for boats and barges. A comparison of figures for several routes in 1792 – Birmingham to Liverpool, Manchester to Birmingham, Chester to Wolverhampton – shows that the cost of sending a ton of goods by canal was between a third and a half of the price of dispatching the same cargo in waggons; these calculations are representative of other long-distance routes [16].

THE DEVELOPMENT OF ROAD TRANSPORT

The development of road transport in the period of early industrialization was rather different from that of the waterways. English roads were long considered to have been in a very poor state by the late seventeenth century; in some areas there had been little improvement for many generations. Traditionally, the upkeep of roads was financed by parishes. The situation was transformed, however, from the mid-seventeenth century onwards by the construction of turnpike roads, which were based on cash payments by users according to complex schedules of tolls. Like canals, turnpikes were constructed after parliamentary authorization was granted and under the supervision of a group of turnpike trustees. There was a spate of building turnpike roads before 1730, but the growth was slow, uneven, and mainly concentrated on the chief arterial routes in and out of London. The national network was consolidated in the quarter-century after 1750, when a 'turnpike mania' occurred with over 500 trusts covering 15,000 miles being established. This was a response to growing prosperity, an increase in passenger and freight traffic, and the 'demonstration effect' of successful turnpiking [195, 196]. By the mid-1770s England and Wales had a thoroughgoing network of turnpiked roads, with their toll gates, tollhouses and gatekeepers, stretching initially outwards from London to all major provincial cities and towns. There was a London to Exeter route, a London to Bristol route (largely the modern A4), and a London to Birmingham route among others. Much turnpiking after 1790 resulted from speculative investment and the spread of the system to northern industrial centres in Yorkshire and Lancashire. By the 1830s over 1,000 turnpike trusts existed, controlling more than 20,000 miles of road and collecting £1.5 million in tolls. They catered for the great upsurge in road traffic that occurred in the late eighteenth and early nineteenth centuries [*Doc. 19*].

Turnpiking was carried out simply with flint and gravel, stone and water, and the cambers of the road surfaces were constructed so that water could drain easily. Before about 1810 little parliamentary legislation dealt with new methods of road-making; the emphasis was rather on restricting the use of the roads in relation to wheels, weights, and carriage construction. 'Macadamizing' the roads, associated with John Loudon McAdam and Thomas Telford, did not occur until the early nineteenth century, when virtually all of the turnpike network had been constructed. These road engineers pioneered cheap and relatively easy solutions to improving road surfaces by specifying the materials needed to repair roads, listing firm administrative guidelines, insisting on regular supervision of repairs, determining the correct degree of convexity of the road surface, and improving drainage.

Turnpike roads were used for transporting goods, passengers and the Royal Mail. Prominent in the transport of goods were the carriers' networks. These were of two kinds: long-haulage carriers covering considerable distances, such as from Southampton to Nottingham or from Bristol to Birmingham; and short-distance carriers, operating in and around market towns and county centres over ten to fifteen miles. The short-distance operators (the village or country carriers) had fixed timetables and ran services between inns in the centre of market towns and the surrounding hinterland. Carriers had covered waggons and carts as their vehicles, pulled by either two or four horses; they took agricultural produce into urban centres and in turn distributed goods available in towns to villages. There were thousands of these carriers operating throughout the century from 1750 to 1850 [202, 214].

In the half-century after about 1780, further improvements to road travel came with the development of the Royal Mail service and higher-speed coaches for passenger travel. Royal Mail coaches were first introduced on the London to Bristol route in 1784. Though numerically small in relation to the public coaching industry, the Mail coaches pioneered new routes, increased speed for vehicles, and operated according to regular, frequent timetables. Moreover, the Royal Mail service stimulated the Post Office to play an active role in road improvement from 1810 onwards [197]. Stagecoaches were more prominent in road travel in the early Industrial Revolution. They achieved notably improved speeds by arranging for regular changes of horses at inns, all-night travel if required over long distances, and use of the turnpike roads. It became customary for stagecoaches to announce their arrival at toll houses by the coaching horn being blown in advance; this was the signal for the turnpike gates to be opened to allow the coaches through without impediment. The record time achieved by a vehicle operating under these conditions on the London to Edinburgh route was 42 hours and 33 minutes in 1830. This was symptomatic of a general change because the speed of road travel throughout the country probably increased by between a third and a fifth between 1750 and 1830 [209].

There were other productivity changes associated with improved road transport. Discounting reduced journey times, recent research suggests that productivity advances came through improved use of horses, economies of scale* such as lower freight costs, and the innovation of fly-waggons such as those used by the firm of Thomas Russell & Company, the main carrier between London and Exeter around 1800. In other words, productivity advances came from better organization rather than extensive new technology. A three-fold productivity increase occurred in long-distance carrying between 1690 and 1840 and a four-fold increase in stage coaching from 1658 to 1820. In both cases, the improvements owed much to better turnpiking of roads [204, 205].

The benefits of improved road transport were not just quantitative. Faster road travel, with lower freight costs, enabled goods to be transported more efficiently from one place to another and over longer distances. Commercial agriculture derived a stimulus from these changes, as local and regional marketing patterns expanded with the filling-in of the road network. Businessmen were able to travel more expeditiously to production centres for industry and raw materials and could therefore take commercial samples with them and acquire better, up-to-date knowledge of shifts in prices. Even shopkeepers in outlying country areas, it seems, were able to tap into these benefits of an improved road network, as regional isolation and self-sufficiency were broken down. Abraham Dent, for instance, a shopkeeper in Kirkby Stephen in the Pennines, apparently tucked away from centres of trade and industry, had customers over a wide area and generally dispatched and received goods on time except for a few times when severe winter weather interrupted services [216]. Seasonal differential charges for freights carried by road were gradually eliminated between 1750 and 1830, which also points indirectly to a regular, reliable service throughout the year. The growth of a provincial newspaper press in the eighteenth century, carrying ever-fuller information on price transactions in different provincial areas, was also tapped by businessmen making use of the road network for better communications.

AN INTEGRATED TRANSPORT NETWORK?

Consideration of waterways and roads in the early Industrial Revolution raises two questions: to what extent was there a unified, national system of internal transport between 1750 and 1830? And was one mode of transport in the vanguard of the other? Certainly, a better nationwide transport system existed in 1830 than in 1750. Canals doubled the number of waterways available for boat and barge traffic and, owing to feats of engineering, were sometimes able to traverse difficult terrain. One thinks, for instance, of the dramatic sequence of locks near Bingley on the Leeds and Liverpool canal or those near Devizes on the Kennet and Avon canal; or of the various tunnels and splendid aqueducts designed by John Rennie, James Brindley and others. A glance at a map of turnpikes will also show a diverse network of roads throughout Britain by the late eighteenth century, with thick criss-crossing near major cities, and penetration into more rugged parts of the provinces.

Of course, road and water transport should not be seen as entirely separate modes of internal communication, though this is often useful for analytical purposes: they were joint aspects of nationwide improvements in internal transport. This can be illustrated by a vignette from the brewing industry: the big London brewers used the River Lea and the River Thames to transport their malt, barley and hops downriver to their city breweries, but at the same time they sent business travellers on the roads into the heart of the barley-growing areas of Hertfordshire and the Thames valley to sample the prices and quality of these raw materials. By this means, speed of communication combined with improved transport costs to stimulate business [169]. This is just one of many examples that could be cited to show that roads and waterways together proved important for the development of regional growth in the early Industrial Revolution.

Canals have traditionally been viewed as being at the forefront of improvements in internal transport in the early industrial age; roads have been accorded less attention. Recent research, however, has raised the profile of improved road transport. Compared with canals, roads were much less expensive to build and maintain; they penetrated even more rough-hewn areas of the country (such as north Wales) than canals; and they did not experience the transit delays caused by a large number of locks (the Leeds and Liverpool canal had 92 locks in 127 miles). Roads did not have the trans-shipment problems that occurred on waterways owing to the different widths of canals and the difficulties of connecting canals to existing rivers (as was the case with the Oxford canal joining the River Thames near Oxford). Another advantage of roads over canals was that they could operate virtually all year round. An ingenious study of data on Lancashire's climate for the period 1771–1831 has shown that, on average, waterways there were inactive for about a month of the year owing to frost, ice and drought, a pattern that was no doubt replicated elsewhere in the country [203]. Thus goods carried by water, although they frequently had cost advantages over commodities carried by road, were subject to more delays and more inactive periods.

THE EMERGENCE OF RAILWAYS

Further improvements to internal transport came with the emergence of railways. The beginnings of the railway network – the 'moving age,' as Thomas Carlyle aptly termed it – lay in the 1830s and 1840s; but there was a 'pre-history' to the emergence of the locomotive. By the turn of the nineteenth century, iron railways were already in use at collieries as a result of improvements in iron smelting with coke. What was lacking was a locomotive. Attempts to design steam-powered locomotives began in earnest in the early nineteenth century with experimentation by engineers such as Richard Trevithick and George and Robert Stephenson, father and son. The first railway to make use of locomotives – albeit over short distances – was the Stockton and Darlington line, in the heart of the north-east coalfield. This opened in 1825 and soon proved successful. It was followed up with an ambitious scheme to construct another railway in the heart of the south Lancashire industrial area. This was the Liverpool-Manchester railway. After Stephenson had won the famous Rainhill trials with his locomotive the *Rocket* in 1829, achieving speeds of 30 m.p.h., the way was clear for the successful development of railways. The Liverpool–Manchester railway opened in 1830 and was an immediate success: it paid shareholders a nearly 10 per cent dividend in its first decade of operation, quickly eliminated competition from stagecoaches between the two cities, and became an important carrier of passengers. Over 400,000 people travelled on this line in its first year of operation [*Doc. 20*].

In the 1830s and 1840s the bulk of the railway network in Britain was constructed. As with canals earlier, there were 'railway manias' – one in 1836–37 and a larger one between 1845 and 1848. In each of these periods credit was readily available for investors in the network. The emergence of provincial stock exchanges at this time, in cities such as Leeds, Liverpool and Manchester, helped to facilitate the railway business. Over 500 miles of railway track were operative by the end of 1838; this figure had increased to 2,000 miles by 1844. By the time of the Great Exhibition in 1851, some 6,000 miles of track had been laid throughout Britain – a figure that had doubled over the five years since 1846. By mid-century the main trunk lines of the railway network had already been established, with services operating between London and most major provincial cities and also between towns and cities in the provinces. Among the famous railway companies established in the two decades between 1830 and 1850 were the Great Western Railway, the Grand Junction Railway, and the Great North of England Railway.

The cost of building the network was considerable: over £40,000 per mile was needed. Money had to be found for rolling stock, locomotives, iron railways, bedded tracks, viaducts, tunnels, and chief engineers' fees. About £250 million had been raised in nominal capital for the railways by 1850. A labour force of some quarter of a million navvies helped to construct the network. Investment in railways accounted for about 6 per cent of national income by the mid-1840s, though modern studies of social savings* have shown that the gap in costs between operating canals and railways was not really all that significant – and certainly less important than the gap in costs between road and water transport [207, 208]. The advantages of railways over existing types of transport lay not so much in costs as in speed, reliability and some other factors discussed below.

THE IMPACT OF RAILWAYS

The early railway network had a number of significant social and economic effects. One was in the speed of travel. Stagecoaches had achieved impressive speeds on turnpike roads by the 1830s. Railways, however, usually operating at speeds of 30 to 40 m.p.h., immediately exceeded the speed of travel achieved by any previous mode of transport. Sydney Smith's comment in 1842 that railways abolished 'time, distance and delay,' was an exaggeration, but it contained a kernel of truth. On the 31-mile journey between Leeds and York in 1840, for instance, coaches took four hours whereas the train ride lasted eighty minutes. Not only was travel time immediately cut over these and other routes; the cost of travel was also cheaper as companies soon became competitive about fares. On the same journey between Leeds and York the cost of an outside seat on a stagecoach was 3s.; the railway fare was initially set at 3s. 6d. and soon reduced to 2s. 6d.

The capacity of the railways for passenger traffic turned out to be an important yet unexpected feature of the new mode of transport. In projecting early railways, it was anticipated that freight would be the main business. But it was not until the 1850s that the railways' earnings from freight exceeded that from passengers. The scale of passenger traffic is indicated by figures for 1850 which show that 73 million people (allowing for more than one trip per person) used the railways and generated a traffic revenue of £6.8 million. Passengers were accommodated in either first-, second- or third-class carriages, the third class being without a roof. Cheap day excursions became availabl e as small travel firms, such as Thomas Cook of Leicester, made use of the railways to run trips to fairs, temperance meetings, fetes and so on. Without the passenger facilities created by railways, the 6 million people visiting the Great Exhibition would have been reduced by five-sixths [212]. The scope for passenger traffic also began to enlarge the potential distance that people could live from their main place of work, as railways witnessed the birth of commuting.

Railways had a significant effect on various industries. Perhaps the most important connection was between the growth of the railway network and the iron industry, for iron was needed for locomotives, rolling stock, track, nails and so forth. And, of course, the iron industry, as we have seen, was intimately connected in its production process with the coal industry. So it is no surprise to find that a lot of railway business was channelled into the industrial sector of south Wales. Railways also had an important link with engineering, not just for the trains themselves but also in the construction of bridges, tunnels and viaducts by celebrated engineers such as Rennie and Isambard Kingdom Brunel. One thinks, for instance, of Brunel's railway bridge across the Tamar, linking Devon with Cornwall, or of Telford's road bridge across the Menai Straits linking Anglesey to the north Wales coast.

The early railway network also had a significant impact on urbanization. Cities such as London, Birmingham, Glasgow and Manchester became very much hubs of the railway network, as John Kellett's book on the impact of railways on Victorian cities amply demonstrates [210]. Within these sprawling urban conglomerations, railway works sprang up in the mid-Victorian period at places such as Gorton in Manchester or Stratford in east London. But, of course, there was also the growth of railway towns. The two best-known of these were Crewe and Swindon. Crewe grew from being a small country parish in Coppenhall, Cheshire in the early 1840s to become the major works of the Liverpool to Birmingham line. 'New' Swindon emerged alongside the market town of Swindon as the major engineering centre for the Great Western Railway on its main route between Paddington and Bristol's Temple Meads.

Railways had a swift and dramatic impact on existing modes of transport. Canals and river navigations soon found themselves outpaced by the railways; they could not compete in terms of speed. Often where freight costs were broadly similar between centres connected by rail and waterways, the rail traffic was easier and speedier. Railways were not subject to some of the major limitations of waterways: they could handle much larger freight, including packages of all shapes and sizes; they were not prone to problems caused by extreme weather; there were no delays comparable to the opening and closing of locks and equalization of water levels on canals. Railways handled a large passenger traffic, which was never possible on waterways. Some rivers and canals, especially in the west Midlands, tried to compete with the rail networks in the 1830s and 1840s; but in nearly every case this was a vain attempt to retain business. Over a thousand miles of waterways, including several major canals, were bought up by existing railway companies in the 1840s in order to destroy their competition. By 1850 river navigations and canals had lost most of their freight business; consequently, many fell into disrepair and disuse. It has taken the efforts of industrial archaeologists in the last decade to resurrect the locks, towpaths and beds of the canals for leisure purposes (as, for instance, on the Kennet and Avon Canal between Reading and Bath).

Part of the road network also suffered badly from the competition provided by the railways. Stagecoaches were immediately affected on the major routes they operated on in the 1830s; they were outpaced in terms of speed and cost. Even where, on paper, costs on stagecoaches looked comparable to railway fares, there were hidden extras in the older mode of travel: tips were expected for the driver and meals had to be added to the fare owing to the longer travelling time [*Doc. 21*]. By 1840 the great stagecoach era had passed. Also by that time the Royal Mail was being transferred to the railways [199]. Carriers' networks on the roads were affected by railway traffic in different ways. Long-distance operators soon found their business hit badly: they could not compete with the railways for the similar services offered. Country carriers, on the other hand, prospered well into the Victorian era and beyond; indeed there were still many village carriers operating with waggons and horses at the outbreak of the First World War. They continued to flourish because they were not in direct competition with the railways: they offered services between urban centres and their hinterlands, taking passengers and goods to and fro over terrain where railways did not penetrate; and they linked up their business increasingly with railway termini [202]. Turnpike roads, however, lost much business to the railways; and it is no surprise to find that the collective revenue of English turnpike trusts fell by one-third between 1837 and 1850. By the mid-Victorian period the steam locomotive had triumphed over traffic on the roads and waterways both in terms of passenger travel and freight haulage.

PART THREE: ASSESSMENT

10 CONCLUSION

This study of Britain's early industrial age has revealed the accelerating pace of economic change in the century between 1750 and 1850. Favoured with good natural resources on a relatively small island, Britain had an advanced pre-industrial economy with significant levels of trading, agricultural and industrial activity before it began to achieve higher rates of economic growth and undergo the gradual structural change from agriculture to industry that characterized the country's early Industrial Revolution. Pre-industrial levels of economic activity had accumulated relatively slowly during long periods when the population was either static or rising and falling modestly in the sixteenth and seventeenth centuries. The challenge for Britain's early industrial economy was different: how to expand production at a time of rapid demographic growth, greater marital fertility and larger families, which exerted more pressure on food resources. Expansion occurred significantly across a broad range of industries, especially textiles, iron and coal. It was sustained by a commercially productive agriculture attuned to innovation in crop rotation and selective livestock breeding and the reorganization of land via the process of parliamentary enclosure. More land was brought into productive use and existing farms cultivated more intensively. Increased cereal and meat yields resulted. Despite some severe harvest crises and years when dearth struck, sufficient food was generally produced to feed the burgeoning population. Combined with the flexibility of rural work patterns in the late eighteenth century and the strong presence of manufacturing in town and countryside before the arrival of factories, wider availability of wage labour provided the economic means for more marriages and for boosting family size and potential earnings: demographically, England experienced a marriage-driven increase in population stimulated more by economic factors than by biological imperatives.

Demographic growth made internal migration more feasible and in some cases necessary. The gradual shift of much of the working population towards industrial and urban work further developed skills in handicraft techniques and, together with the advent of new machinery, provided the impetus for the reorganization of textile production into mills. Whether proto-industrialization underpinned the move from domestic industry to factories is still a problematic proposition given the problems of timing, capital transfer and demographic issues related to the theory. But the fact that some forms of cottage industry continued to flourish until well into the nineteenth century gave the British manufacturing economy a solid and flexible basis of artisan skills as well as providing regular work for men, women and children. Such skills were also in evidence in the inventiveness of engineers, craftsmen and entrepreneurs in developing new techniques of iron and steel production and improved steam engines to increase coal output. Industrial growth was achieved partly by the application of new techniques and machines and their diffusion throughout the economy but also by labour productivity resulting from more intense and longer hours of work and the contribution of family units to the work process.

The transition from an advanced organic economy to one based on mineral fuel technology, though elongated in time, gave Britain a crucial advantage over its main economic rivals in the late eighteenth century. Moreover, unlike those competitors France and the Netherlands, in Britain there was not the spectre of political revolution to impede economic progress in the period 1780–1800 when aggregate demand increased throughout the British economy. When war interrupted economic activity seriously, as in the long years of conflict with revolutionary and Napoleonic France, British industry, trade and agriculture generally overcame the problem, even though the economic victory, like the military one, was hard won. The state did not play a leading role in promoting Britain's early industrial economy, but it gathered excise and other taxes that yielded the funds to protect the nation in wartime. Indirectly, many areas of economic activity depended on tacit support from parliamentary legislation; this is as true of turnpike roads and canal companies as of parliamentary enclosure. In addition, 22 years of war with France (1793–1815) witnessed other help from the state to ensure that rates of economic growth did not plummet: generous Poor Law provision to help cases of genuine hardship, and raising of income tax to support the war effort.

Entrepreneurial drive was another prominent feature of Britain's early industrialization. It was evident not just in the commercial improvement of agriculture, factory organization and the development of mineral fuel technology, but also in improvements to the organization of trade and transport. The growth of turnpike roads and the spread of canals increased the internal arteries of communication throughout the nation, helping to integrate the resources of localities and regions as never before, a process carried a stage further by the rapid growth of the early railway network. Railways also stimulated passenger traffic on an extensive scale. British foreign trade increased greatly in volume and value, and ports and docks were built or extended to cope with growing commerce. Significant advances occurred in the deployment of credit, the settlement of payments and commercial knowledge, all of which enhanced business expertise and helped to circulate commodities from their point of production to their place of consumption. Distribution of goods and services, both at home and abroad, improved in the early industrial age as new methods of commercial organization came to the fore. Facilities for investment and borrowing also became more intricate with the growth of the banking network, the emergence of stock exchanges, and the rise of fire and marine insurance. Though this book has looked at different components of the economy in separate chapters, perhaps the hallmark of economic life in early industrial Britain lay in the complementarities between the different sectors and their integration into a more nationwide network of business and finance over the century after 1750.

Despite experiencing more gradual economic growth between 1750 and 1850 than was once thought, dramatic changes had still occurred to emphasize that Britain did undergo the birth of an Industrial Revolution in that century. Admittedly, there was still much traditional rural labour and domestic industry in the mid-Victorian era, plus margins of the nation where time had stood still. There were also areas of deindustrialization, labour immobility and poverty. But it would be misleading to suggest that Britain's early Industrial Revolution was therefore a myth, that continuity outweighed the dynamics of change. Compared with 1750, Britain by 1850 had several large industrial cities with flourishing hinterlands, a vastly improved internal communications network, more efficiently organized agriculture, more sophisticated business techniques in overseas trade, financial institutions that in many cases still exist today, ongoing evidence of inventiveness and technological ingenuity, more intensive economic development in regions with good fuel resources and raw materials, and a reputation for producing quality manufactured goods at cheaper prices than most of her competitors.

These economic improvements carried a price. Many workers faced difficulties in securing job protection in a world where living standards could be precarious and few ordinary men, let alone women, had political enfranchisement in a nation where the landed elite maintained considerable power. The companion to this volume, *The Birth of Industrial Britain: Social Change 1750–1850,* analyses the complex social consequences of the economic changes that have been discussed in this book, in order to assess the benefits and costs of industrialization on the first generations of people who experienced the dislocation caused by such a significant transition. These consequences are traced in patterns of work and leisure, in religious and educational change, and in standards of living, to demonstrate the implications of Britain's early Industrial Revolution for the mass of ordinary people who built it.

PART FOUR: DOCUMENTS

DOCUMENT 1 MALTHUS ON POPULATION GROWTH

The Revd Thomas Malthus (1766–1834) pioneered the study of demographic history. The preventive and positive checks to population growth, outlined in this extract, still inform analysis of the reasons lying behind population growth and decline, two centuries after Malthus formulated his principles.

(a) *The principle of population*
I think it will be allowed, that no state has hitherto existed (at least that we have any account of) where the manners were so pure and simple, and the means of subsistence so abundant, that no check whatever has existed to early marriages; among the lower classes, from a fear of not providing well for their families; or among the higher classes, from a fear of lowering their condition in life. Consequently in no state that we have yet known, has the power of population been left to exert with perfect freedom.

Whether the law of marriage be instituted, or not, the dictate of nature and virtue, seems to be an early attachment to one woman. Supposing a liberty of changing in the case of an unfortunate choice, this liberty would not affect population till it arose to a height greatly vicious; and we are now supposing the existence of a society where vice is scarcely known.

In a state therefore of great equality and virtue, where pure and simple manners prevailed, and where the means of subsistence were so abundant, that no part of the society could have any fears about providing amply for a family, the power of population being left to exert itself unchecked, the increase of the human species would evidently be much greater than any increase that has been hitherto known.

In the United States of America, where the means of subsistence have been more ample, the manners of the people more pure, and consequently the checks to early marriages fewer, than in any of the modern states of Europe, the population has been found to double itself in twenty-five years.

This ratio of increase, though short of the utmost power of population, yet as the result of actual experience, we will take it as our rule; and say,

That population, when unchecked, goes on doubling itself every twenty-five years, or increases in a geometrical ratio.

Let us now take any spot of earth, this island for instance, and see in what ratio the subsistence it affords can be supposed to increase. We will begin with it under its present state of cultivation.

If I allow that by the best possible policy, by breaking up more land, and by great encouragements to agriculture, the produce of this island may be doubled in the first twenty-five years, I think it will be allowing as much as any person can well demand.

In the next twenty-five years, it is impossible to suppose that the produce could be quadrupled. It would be contrary to all our knowledge of the qualities of land. The very utmost that we can conceive, is, that the increase in the second twenty-five years might equal the present produce. Let us then take this for our rule, though certainly far beyond the truth; and allow that by great exertion, the whole produce of the island might be increased every twenty-five years, by a quantity of subsistence equal to what it at present produces. The most enthusiastic speculator cannot suppose a greater increase than this. In a few centuries it would make every acre of land in the island like a garden.

Yet this ratio of increase is evidently arithmetical.

It may be fairly said, therefore, that the means of subsistence increase in an arithmetical ratio.

(b) *The preventive check*

In examining the principal states of modern Europe, we shall find, that though they have increased very considerably in population since they were nations of shepherds, yet that, at present, their progress is but slow; and instead of doubling their numbers every twenty-five years, they require three or four hundred years, or more, for that purpose. Some, indeed, may be absolutely stationary, and others even retrograde. The cause of this slow progress in population cannot be traced to a decay of the passion between the sexes. We have sufficient reason to think that this natural propensity exists still in undiminished vigour. Why then do not its effects appear in a rapid increase of the human species? An intimate view of the state of society in any one country in Europe, which may serve equally for all, will enable us to answer this question, and to say, that a foresight of the difficulties attending the rearing of a family, acts as preventive check; and the actual distresses of some of the lower classes, by which they are disabled from giving the proper food and attention to their children, acts as a positive check, to the natural increase of population.

(c) *The positive check*

The positive check to population, by which I mean, the check that represses an increase which is already begun, is confined chiefly, though not perhaps solely, to the lowest orders of society. This check is not so obvious to common view as the other I have mentioned; and, to prove distinctly the force and extent of its operation, would require, perhaps, more data than we are in possession of. But I believe it has been very generally remarked by those who have attended to bills of mortality, that of the number of children who die annually, much too great a proportion belongs to those, who may be supposed unable to give their offspring proper food and attention; exposed as they are occasionally to severe distress, and confined, perhaps to unwholesome habitations and hard labour. This mortality among the children of the poor has been constantly taken notice of in all towns. It certainly does not prevail in an equal degree in the country; but the subject has not hitherto received sufficient attention to enable any one to say, that there are not more deaths in proportion, among the children of the poor, even in the country, than among those of the middling and higher classes. Indeed, it seems difficult to suppose that a labourer's wife who has six children, and who is sometimes in absolute want of bread, should be able always to give them the food and attention necessary to support life.

Thomas R. Malthus, *An Essay on Population*, 1st edn 1798 [9, *pp. 179–81*].

DOCUMENT 2   THE NORFOLK ROTATION OF CROPS, 1787

An explanation of one of the main sources of agricultural productivity in eighteenth-century England.

In Norfolk, as in other arable countries, husbandmen vary more or less in the succession of crops and fallows to each other – but if we confine ourselves to *this* District; the north-east quarter of the country; we may venture to assert, without hazard, that no other District of equal extent in the kingdom is so invariable in this respect; commonfield Districts excepted.

It is highly probable, that a principal part of the lands of this District have been kept invariably, for at least a century past, under the following course of cultivation.

Wheat
Barley
Turnips
Barley
Clover

Rye grass, broken up about Midsummer, and fallowed for wheat, in rotation. Thus, supposing a farm to be laid-out, with nineteen or twenty arable divisions, of nearly equal size, and these to be brought into six regular shifts, each shift would consist of three pieces; with a piece or two in reserve, at liberty to be cropped with oats, peas, tares, buck; or to receive a thorough cleansing by a whole-year's fallow.

This course of culture is well adapted to the soil of this District, which is much more productive of barley than of wheat; and is in every other respect, as will hereafter appear, admirably adapted to that excellent system of management of which it is the basis.

The soil of the southern parts of the District being stronger and deeper than that upon which the foregoing course of crops is prevalent, it is better suited to wheat; and there the round of

Wheat
Turnips
Barley
Clover

is common; though not in universal practice.

This difference in soil and management renders it necessary to consider the southern Hundreds of Fleg, South-Walsham, and Blowfield, as appendages, rather than as parts, of the District most immediately under description: which is furnished with a less genial soil; namely, that shallow, and somewhat lightish, sandy loam, which may be called the common covering of the county; broken, however, in some places, by a richer, stronger, deeper soil; and in others, by barren heaths and unproductive sands; from which even the Hundreds of Erpingham, Turnstead, and Happing, are not entirely free; though, perhaps, they enjoy a greater uniformity of soil than any other District of equal extent in the county.

This therefore, is the site best adapted to the study of the system of management which has raised the name of Norfolk husbandmen, and which is still preserved, inviolate, in this secluded District. For a shallow sandy loam, no matter whether it lie in Norfolk or in any other part of the kingdom, there cannot, perhaps, be devised a better course of culture; or, taken all in all, a better system of management, than that which is here in universal practice.

But excellent as this succession of crops undoubtedly is, it cannot be invariably kept up; for even a Norfolk husbandmen cannot command a crop of turnips or a crop of clover; and when either of these fail, the regularity of the succession is of course broken into.

If his turnips disappoint him, he either lets his land lie fallow through the winter, and sows it with barley, in course, in the spring; or more frequently though less judiciously, sows it with wheat in the autumn; sometimes, though not always, sowing it with clover and rye grass in the spring; by this means regaining his regular course.

If the clover miss, the remedy is more difficult; and no general rule is in this case observed. Sometimes a crop of peas is taken the first year; and the next, buck plowed under; or perhaps a crop of oats are taken the first year, and over these clover sown for the second: in either of these cases, the soil comes round for wheat the third year, in due succession.

It has already appeared in the *Heads of a Lease* p. 75, that the Norfolk farmers are restricted from taking more than two crops of corn successively. At the close of a lease this restriction may sometimes have a good effect; for ill-blood between the landlord and tenant too frequently leads a farmer to do what he knows will, in the end, be injurious both to himself and his farm. The crime of taking more than two crops of corn in successively is, however, held by farmers in general, in an odious light, and is never practised by a good farmer, unless 'to bring into course' a small patch, with some adjoining piece; – or to regulate his shifts.

William Marshall, *The Rural Economy of Norfolk Comprising the Management of Landed Estates and the Present Practice of Agriculture in that County*, 2 vols, London, 1787, 1, pp. 132–6.

DOCUMENT 3   THE ADVANTAGES OF PARLIAMENTARY ENCLOSURE

Written at a time when parliamentary enclosure was at its height, this extract emphasizes the advantages of enclosing land for livestock rearing, drainage and agricultural employment.

Inclosing – The benefits and advantages that would be derived from a general inclosure of commons, are so numerous, as far to exceed my powers of description or computation. The opportunity it would afford, of separating dry ground from wet, or well draining the latter, and liming the rotten parts, is of infinite consequence: as such an arrangement would, with the aid of intelligent breeders, be the means of raising a breed of sheep and neat cattle, far superior to the present race of wretched half starved animals now seen in such situations. It would have the effect of supporting a more numerous stock, upon the same quantity of food, by restraining the cattle and sheep within in due bounds. Their restless and rambling disposition, not only treads the grass off the ground, but also takes the flesh off their bones. This renders the attendance of a shepherd necessary, and requires likewise that they be driven to and from the fold. Further, the live stock would by this means be rendered many hundreds per cent more valuable to individuals and the community, than it has hitherto been, or can possibly be, without inclosure: and, *what is of the last, the greatest importance, it would tend to preserve such improved breed from that destructive malady, the rot, which makes such terrible havock among our flocks.* Add to this, that the markets would be more plentifully supplied with beef and mutton, and the price of these articles considerably reduced ...

The commons of this kingdom being, with very few exceptions, without ridges, furrows, or drains, have not the means of discharging that superfluous water from the surface of them, which is well known to be of great detriment to vegetation in general. Many commons on low situations, and where the soil happens to be of a retentive quality, hold water like a sponge, which being always stagnant, as well as excessive in quantity, renders the soil of such doubt, the cause of many of the disorders which that animal is subject to, particularly that fatal malady the rot. From the same causes also, the neighbourhood of such commons must be particularly unfriendly to the health and longevity of man. Only let us reverse the scene, and for a moment suppose these commons to be inclosed, the necessary ditches and drains sunk, and the land brought into tillage, and we shall see all the superabundant moisture got rid of; and the water, being kept in constant motion, by trickling down the sides of the ridges into the furrows, and from thence, into the ditches and rivulets, will be found to fertilise the very soil which, in its present stagnant state, it serves to injure: while, by leaving the land dry, it will be rendered more healthy both for men and cattle. The effects of such a measure would soon shew themselves in many districts of this island, which at present, are very unpropitious to the health of man, in the much greater longevity of the inhabitants.

It may farther be observed, that commons are entirely defective in the great article of labour; but no sooner does an inclosure take place, than the scene is agreeably changed from a dreary waste, to the more pleasing one of the same spot appearing all animation, activity and bustle. Every man, capable of performing such operations, is furnished with plenty of employment, in sinking ditches and drains, in making banks and hedges, and in planting quicks and trees. Nor are the wheelwright, carpenter, smith, and other rural artificers, under the necessity of being idle spectators of the scene, since abundance of work will be found for them, in the erection of farmhouses, and the necessary appendages thereto; and in the forming and making roads, bridges, gates, stiles, implements of husbandry, etc. Even after a few years, when these kind of temporary exertions are over, by the whole being brought into a regular system of husbandry, it will still continue to provide both food and employment for a very increased population.

John Middleton, *View of the Agriculture of Middlesex*, 1798 [9, *pp. 82–3*].

DOCUMENT 4   THE EFFECTS OF ENCLOSURE ON THE POOR

Argues that engrossing land and raising rents came with parliamentary enclosure and that a peasantry was deprived of access to land as a consequence. The results, it is suggested, were a rise in sporadic hired labour by the day and the increase of rural poverty.

The practice of enlarging and engrossing of farms, and especially that of depriving the peasantry of all landed property, have contributed greatly to increase the number of dependent poor.

1. The land-owner, to render his income adequate to the increased expense of living, unites several small farms into one, raises the rent to the utmost, and avoids the expense of repairs. The rich farmer also engrosses as many farms as he is able to stock; lives in more credit and comfort than he could otherwise do; and out of the profits of the several farms, makes an ample provision for one family. Thus thousands of families, which formerly gained an independent livelihood on those separate farms, have been gradually reduced to the class of day labourers. But day labourers are some-

times in want of work, and are sometimes unable to get work; and in either case their resort is the parish. It is a fact, that thousands of parishes have not now half the numbers of farmers which they had formerly. And in proportion as the number of farming families has decreased, the number of poor families has increased.

2. The depriving the peasantry of all landed property has beggared multitudes. It is plainly agreeable to sound policy, that as many individuals as possible in a state should possess an interest in the soil; because this attaches them strongly to the country and its constitution, and makes them zealous and resolute in defending them. But the gentry of this kingdom seem to have lost sight of this wise and salutary policy. Instead of giving to labouring people a valuable stake in the soil, the opposite measure has so long prevailed, that but few cottages, comparatively, have now any land about them. Formerly many of the lower sort of people occupied tenements of their own with parcels of land about them, or they rented such of others. On these they raised for themselves a considerable part of their subsistence, without being obliged, as now, to buy all they want at shops. And this kept numbers from coming to the parish. But since those small parcels of ground have been swallowed up in the contiguous farms and enclosures, and the cottages themselves have been pulled down; the families which used to occupy them are crowded together in decayed farm houses, with hardly ground enough about them for a cabbage garden: and being thus reduced to be mere hirelings, they are of course very liable to come to want. And not only the men occupying those tenements, but their wives and children too, could formerly, when they wanted work abroad, employ themselves, profitably at home; whereas now, few of these are constantly employed, except in harvest; so that almost the whole burden of providing for their families rests upon the men. Add to this, that the former occupiers of small farms and tenements, though poor themselves, gave away something in alms to their poorer neighbours; a resource which is not much diminished.

Thus an amazing number of people have been reduced from a comfortable state of partial independence to the precarious conditions of hirelings, who, when out of work, must immediately come to their parish. And the great plenty of working hands always to be had when wanted, having kept the price of labour below its proper level, the consequence is universally felt in the increased number of dependent poor.

Revd D. Davies, *The Case of the Labourers in Husbandry*, 1795 [14, *pp. 64–5*].

DOCUMENT 5   ADAM SMITH ON THE DIVISION OF
              LABOUR

*A classic discussion of the division of labour in manufacturing by the author
of* The Wealth of Nations, *a highly influential work on economic policy that
argued for freedom in economic enterprise. By choosing the pinmaking trade
to illustrate his general point, Smith underscored the significance of small-scale
manufacturing processes during Britain's early period of industrialization.*

The greatest improvement in the productive powers of labour, and the greater
part of the skill, dexterity and judgement with which it is anywhere directed,
or applied, seem to have been the effects of the division of labour.

The effects of the division of labour, in the general business of society, will
be more easily understood by considering in what manner it operates in some
particular manufactures. It is commonly supposed to be carried furthest in
some very trifling ones; not perhaps that it really is carried further in them
than in others of more importance; but in those trifling manufactures which
are destined to supply the small wants of but a small number of people, the
whole number of workmen must necessarily be small; and those employed in
every different branch of the work can often be collected into the same workhouse, and placed at once under the view of the spectator. In those great manufactures on the contrary, which are destined to supply the great wants of the
great body of the people, every different branch of the work employs so great
a number of workmen that it is impossible to collect them all into the same
workhouse. We can seldom see more, at one time, than those employed in one
single branch. Though in such manufactures, therefore, the work may really
be divided into a greater number of parts than in those of a more trifling
nature, the division is not near so obvious, and has accordingly been much
less observed.

To take an example, therefore, from a very trifling manufacture: but one in
which the division of labour has been very often taken notice of, the trade of
the pin-maker; a workman not educated to this business (which the division
of labour has rendered a distinct trade), nor acquainted with the use of the
machinery employed in it (to the invention of which the same division of
labour has probably given occasion), could scarce, perhaps, with his utmost
industry, make one pin in a day, and certainly could not make twenty. But in
the way in which this business is now carried on, not only the whole work is a
peculiar trade, but it is divided into a number of branches, of which the
greater part are likewise peculiar trades. One man draws out the wire,
another straights it, a third cuts it, a fourth points it, a fifth grinds it at the
tope for receiving the head; to make the head requires two or three distinct
operations; to put it on is a peculiar business, to whiten the pins is another; it
is even a trade by itself to put them into the paper; and the important business
of making a pin is, in this manner, divided into about eighteen distinct operations, which, in some manufactories, are all performed by distinct hands,

though in others the same man will sometimes perform two or three of them. I have seen a small manufactory of this kind where ten men only were employed, and where some of them consequently performed two or three distinct operations. But though they were very poor, and therefore but indifferently accommodated with the necessary machinery, they could, when they exerted themselves, make among them twelve pounds of pins in a day. There are in a pound upwards of four thousand pins of a middling size. Those ten persons, therefore, could make among them upwards of forty eight thousand pins in a day. Each person, therefore, making a tenth part of forty eight thousand pins, might be considered as making four thousand eight hundred pins in a day. But if they had all wrought separately and independently, and without any of them having been educated to this peculiar business, they certainly could not each of them have made twenty, perhaps not one pin in a day; that is, certainly, not the two hundred and fortieth, perhaps not the four thousand eight hundredth part of what they are at present capable of performing, in consequence of a proper division and combination of their operations.

[5, vol. 1 *pp. 13–16*].

DOCUMENT 6   THE DOMESTIC WOOLLEN INDUSTRY AND THE YORKSHIRE CLOTH HALLS

Outlines the processes involved in the manufacture, sale and distribution of woollen cloth in one of its leading production centres.

In the last-mentioned, or Domestic system, which is that of Yorkshire, the Manufacture is conducted by a multitude of Master Manufacturers, generally possessing a very small, and scarcely ever any great extent of Capital. They buy the Wool of the Dealer; and, in their own houses, assisted by their wives and children, and from two or three to six or seven Journeymen, they dye it (when dying is necessary) and through all the different stages work it up into undressed Cloth.

Various processes however, the chief of which were formerly done by hand, under the Manufacturer's own roof, are now performed by Machinery, in public Mills, as they are called, which work for hire. There are several such Mills near every manufacturing Village, so that the Manufacturer, with little inconvenience or loss of time, carries thither his goods, and fetches them back again when the process is completed. When it has attained to the state of undressed Cloth, he carries it on the Market-day to a public Hall or Market, where the Merchants repair to purchase.

Several thousands of these small Master Manufacturers attend the Market of Leeds, where there are three Halls for the exposure and sale of their Cloths: and there are other similar Halls, where the same system of selling in public Market prevails, at Bradford, Halifax, and Huddersfield. The Halls consist of long walks or galleries, throughout the whole length of which the Master Manufacturers stand in a double row, each behind his own little division or stand, as it is termed, on which his goods are exposed to sale. In the interval between these rows the Merchants pass along, and make their purchases. At the end of an hour, on the ringing of a bell, the Market closes, and such Cloths as have been purchased are carried home to the Merchants houses: such Goods as remain unsold continuing in the Halls till they find a purchaser at some ensuing Market. It should however be remarked, that a practice has also obtained of later years, of Merchants giving out Samples to some Manufacturer whom they approve, which Goods are brought to the Merchant directly, without ever coming into the Halls. These however, no less than the others, are manufactured by him in his own family. The greater Merchants have their working-room, or, as it is termed, their Shop, in which their Workmen, or, as they are termed, Croppers, all work together. The Goods which, as it has been already stated, are bought in the undressed state, here undergo various processes, till, being completely finished, they are sent away for the use of the consumer, either in the Home or the Foreign Market; the Merchants sending them abroad directly with-out the intervention of any other Factor. Sometimes again the Goods are dressed at a stated rate by Dressers, who take them in for that purpose.

The greater part of the Domestic Clothiers live in Villages and detached houses, covering the whole face of a district of from 20 to 30 miles in length, and from 12 to 15 in breadth. Coal abounds throughout the whole of it; and a great proportion of the Manufacturers occupy a little Land, from 3 to 12 or 15 acres each. They often likewise keep a Horse, to carry their Cloth to the Fulling Mill and the Market.

Report from the Committee on the Woollen Industry, Parliamentary Papers, 1806 [143, p. 80].

DOCUMENT 7   TECHNOLOGY IN THE COTTON INDUSTRY: THE DEVELOPMENT OF THE SPINNING MULE

An explanation of the working of the spinning machinery that transformed the cotton industry in the early Industrial Revolution, with particular reference to Samuel Crompton's invention of a 'mule'. The extract also emphasizes the quality of the yarn produced and the reduction in the cost of raw cotton fibre.

During the period that has now passed under review, Hargreaves and Arkwright had established the Cotton Manufacture by their spinning machines; but those machines were not adapted for the finer qualities of yarn. The water-frame spun twist for warps, but it could not be advantageously used for the finer qualities, as thread of great tenuity has not strength to bear the pull of the rollers when winding itself on the bobbins. This defect in the spinning machinery was remedied by the invention of another machine, called the *Mule*, or the *Mule Jenny*, from its combining the principles of Arkwright's water-frame and Hargreave's jenny. Like the former, it has a system of rollers to reduce the roving; and, like the latter, it has spindles without bobbins to give the twist, and the thread is stretched and spun at the same time by the spindles, after the rollers have ceased to give out the rove. The distinguishing feature of the mule is, that the spindles, instead of being stationary, as in both the other machines, are placed on a moveable carriage, which is wheeled out to the distance of fifty-four or fifty six inches from the roller-beam, in order to stretch and twist the thread, and wheeled in again to wind it on the spindles. In the jenny, the clasp, which held the rovings, was drawn back by the hand from the spindles; in the mule, on the contrary, the spindles recede from the clasp, or from the roll-beam which acts as a clasp. The rollers of the mule draw out the roving much less than those of the water-frame; and they act like the clasp of the jenny, by stopping and holding fast the rove, after a certain quantity has been given out, whilst the spindles continue to recede for a short distance further; so that the draught on the thread is in part made by the receding of the spindles. By this arrangement, comprising the advantages of both the rollers and the spindles, the thread is stretched more gently and equably, and a much finer quality of yarn can therefore be produced.

This excellent machine, which has superseded the jenny, and to a considerable extent the water-frame, and which has carried the cotton manufacture to a perfection it could not otherwise have attained, was invented by Samuel Crompton, a weaver, of respectable character and moderate circumstances, living at Hall-in-the-Wood, near Bolton. The date of the invention has been generally stated to be 1775, but ... he says in a letter to a friend 'In regard to the mule, the date of its being first completed was in the year 1779: at the end of the following year I was under the necessity of making it public, or destroying it, as it was not in my power to keep it and work it, and to destroy it was too painful a task, having been four and a half years, at least, wherein every moment of time and power of mind, as well as expense, which my other employment would permit, were devoted to this one end, the having good yarn to weave; so that to destroy it, I could not'. Being of a retiring and unambitious disposition, he took out no patent, and only regretted that public curiosity would not allow him 'to enjoy his little invention to himself in his garret', and to earn, by his own manual labour, undisturbed, the fruits of his ingenuity and perseverance. The very superior quality of his yarn drew persons from all quarters, to ascertain the means whereby he produced it. He stated to Mr Bannatyne, that on the invention of his machine 'he obtained 14s. per lb. for the spinning and preparation of No. 40, (ie. yarn weighing 40 hanks to the pound) that after a short time after, he got 25s. per lb. for the spinning and preparation of No. 60; and that he then spun a small quantity of No. 80, to show that it was not impossible, as was supposed, to spin yarn of so fine a grist; and for the spinning and preparation of this he got 42s. per lb.'

These prices were commanded by the unrivalled excellence of the yarn; and it affords a criterion to estimate the value of the machine, when it is found that the price of yarn No. 100 is at the present day only 2s. 3d. to 3s. per lb. including the cost of the raw material, which is 10d. or 1s. – this surprising reduction having been effected chiefly by the powers of the mule; and that, whereas it was before supposed impossible to spin eighty hanks to the pound, as many as *three hundred and fifty* hanks to the pound have since been spun, each hank measuring 840 yards, and forming together a thread of a hundred and sixty seven miles in length!

Edward Baines, *The History of the Cotton Manufacture in Great Britain*, 1835 [14, *pp. 34–5*].

DOCUMENT 8   INDUSTRIAL DISCIPLINE 1797 AND 1817

A typical example of the fines meted out for misdemeanours in the early factories.

The horrid and impious Vice of profane CURSING and SWEARING – and the Habits of Losing Time – and DRUNKENNESS – are become so frequent and notorious; that unless speedily checked, they may justly provoke the Divine Vengeance to increase the Calamities these Nations now labour under.

NOTICE is hereby given,
That all the Hands in the Service of
SAMUEL OLDKNOW
working in his Mill, or elsewhere, must be subject to the following
RULE:

That when any person, either Man, Woman or Child, is heard to CURSE or SWEAR, the same shall forfeit One Shilling – And when any Hand is absent from Work (unless unavoidably detained by Sickness, or Leave being first obtained), the same shall forfeit as many Hours of Work as have been lost; and if by the Job or Piece, after the rate of 2s. 6d. per Day, Such Forfeitures to be put into a Box, and distributed to the Sick and Necessitous, at the discretion of their employer.
MELLOR, 1st December, 1797

George Unwin *et al.*, *Samuel Oldknow and the Arkwrights: The Industrial Revolution at Stockport and Marple*, Manchester University Press, 1924, p. 198.

DOCUMENT 9   LETTER FROM WILLIAM MILNES TO SIR
JOSEPH BANKS, 22 DECEMBER 1811, ON
FRAME-BRAKING BY LUDDITES

An account of the damage to stocking-frame machinery in the Nottingham-shire hosiery industry by the followers of the mythical Ned Ludd.

Ashover, 22 December, 1811.

I am extremely sorry to inform you that the stocking frame-breaking system which has caused so much alarm and disturbance in the neighbourhood of Nottingham has extended its baneful effects into this neighbourhood. At Pentridge, about six miles from hence, a person of the name of Topham has had frames destroyed to the amount of £500. ... Two men came to this place who called themselves inspectors from the committee; they went to every stockinger's house and discharged them from working under such prices as they gave them a list of, and said they should come again in a few days, and in case any of them were found working without having a ticket from their master saying that he was willing to give the prices stated in their list, they should break their frames. They summoned all the stockingers, about 12 or 14 in number of master men to a public house with as much consequence as if they had had a mandate from the Prince Regent. When they got them hither, all I can learn at present, was for the purpose of collecting money from them for the support of those families who were deprived of getting their bread by having their frames broken. Where they found a frame worked by a person who had not served a regular apprenticeship, or by a woman, they discharged them from working, and if they promised to do so, they stuck a paper upon the frame with these words written on it – 'Let this frame stand, the colts removed' – colt is the name given to all those who have not served a regular apprenticeship.

[9, *pp.* 140–1]

DOCUMENT 10   **STEAM POWER**

A contemporary description of the benefits of the Watt steam engine to the early industrial economy.

There are many engines made by Bolton and Watt, forty years ago, which have continued in constant work all that time with very slight repairs. What a multitude of valuable horses would have been worn out in doing the service of these machines! and what a vast quantity of grain would they have consumed! Had British industry not been aided by Watt's invention it must have done with a retarding pace in consequence of the increasing cost of motive power, and would, long ere now, have experienced in the price of horses, and scarcity of waterfalls, an insurmountable barrier to further advancement, could horses, even at the low prices to which their rival, steam, has kept them, be employed to drive a cotton mill at the present day, they would devour all the profits of the manufacturer.

Steam engines furnish the means not only of their support but of their multiplication. They create a vast demand for fuel; and, while they lend their powerful arms to drain the pits and to raise the coals, they call into employment multitudes of miners, engineers, ship builders and sailors, and cause the construction of canals and railways; and while they enable these rich fields of industry to be cultivated to the utmost, they leave thousands of fine arable fields free for the production of food to man, which must otherwise have been allotted to the food of horses. Steam engines, moreover, by the cheapness and steadiness of their action, fabricate cheap goods, and procure in their exchange a liberal supply of the necessaries and comforts of life, produced in foreign lands.

A. Ure, *The Philosophy of Manufactures,* 1835, p. 29.

DOCUMENT 11   COALBROOKDALE

Outlines the use of coke to smelt iron at the famous Shropshire ironworks owned by the Quaker Darby family. The varied uses of the cast iron produced are emphasized.

We decamped with Abraham Darby to take a general Survey of the Furnaces, Forges, and other Conveniences for the manufactury of Iron. The Ore is brought a few Miles from the mine to the works. It is then laid on a great Pile with a Stratum of Coal under it, and a considerable Quantity of loose pieces thrown into the general mess. These coals are lighted and thus the Ore is first calcined, being purged of a variety of combustible materials before it is taken to the Furnace. The Coal for this business, as well as for the principal Concerns of these works, is burnt into Charcoal before it is used. For this purpose it is thrown up into a multitude of uniform hillocks and attended till it become of a proper Quality for their Use. The Coals are brought by Land 2 or 3 Miles on fine level Iron paved Roads. Down the declivities they use no horses. By the same Roads the Lime and Ore are also conveyed.

The old Furnace (nearest the house) has been in blast without the least diminution for 7 years past. It continues to vomit out its Flames and emit a vast Column of Smoak. The great Number of Buildings for the Furnaces, Forges, Founderies, Warehouses &c and the habitations of the Workman 200 of whom are imployed compose a little City. It is astonishing to think of the uses to which Cast Iron is converted. Besides common castings they make their Chimney Tops, their Window Cases, their Chimney Pieces, their Sashes, their floors, their Scantlen for their Roofs, Doors Pallisadoes, Ploughshares, beside an hundred other Utensils for domestic Use of this permanent and durable material. The Arch over one of their door Cases which is 16 feet in

Diameter is likewise of Cast Iron. But all these are trifling compared with the great Tools for which they have occasion in the progress of their Business. Their Boilers and Cylinders and above all, their Conduits for water to turn the Mills which they serve instead of Races, and answer much better, as less Water is wasted both by the exhalations of the Sun, and what Ground would absorb. All these are of Cast Iron.

Travel Journal of Jabez Fisher, 1776 [12, p. 265].

DOCUMENT 12   **ADAM SMITH ON CAPITAL ACCUMULATION**

Puts forward the view that frugality and savings were the prime source of capital accumulation, at the same time expressing disdain for funds frittered away in consumption.

Capitals are increased by parsimony, and diminished by prodigality and misconduct.

Whatever a person saves from his revenue he adds to his capital, and either employs it himself in maintaining an additional number of productive hands, or enables some other person to do so, by lending it to him for an interest, that is, for a share of the profits. As the capital of an individual can be increased only by what he saves from his annual revenue or his annual gains, so the capital of a society, which is the same with that of all individuals who compose it, can be increased only in the same manner.

Parsimony, and not industry, is the immediate cause of the increase of capital. Industry, indeed, provides the subject which parsimony accumulates. But whatever industry might acquire, if parsimony did not save and store up, the capital would never be the greater.

Parsimony, by increasing the fund which is destined for the maintenance of productive hands, tends to increase the number of those hands whose labour adds to the value of the subject upon which it is bestowed. It tends, therefore, to increase the exchangeable value of the annual produce of the land and labour of the country. It puts into motion an additional quantity of industry, which gives an additional value to the annual produce.

What is annually saved is as regularly consumed as what is annually spent, and nearly in the same time too; but it is consumed by a different set of people. That portion of his revenue which a rich man annually spends, is, in most cases, consumed by idle guests and menial servants, who leave nothing behind them in return for their consumption. That portion which he annually saves, as for the sake of profit, it is immediately employed as a capital, is consumed in the same manner, and nearly in the same time too, but by different set of people; by labourers, manufacturers, and artificers, who reproduce with a profit, the value of their annual consumption. His revenue, we shall suppose, is paid him in money. Had he spent the whole, the food, clothing, and lodging, which the whole could have purchased, would have been distributed among the former set of people. By saving a part of it, as that part is, for the sake of the profit, immediately employed as a capital, either by himself or by some other person, the food, clothing, and lodging, which may be purchased with it, are necessarily reserved for the latter. The consumption is the same, but the consumers are different.

By what a frugal man annually saves, he not only affords maintenance to an additional number of productive hands, for that or the ensuing year, but like the founder of a public workhouse, he establishes, as it were, a perpetual fund for the maintenance of an equal number in all times to come. The perpetual allotment and destination of this fund, indeed, is not always guarded by any positive law, by any trust right or deed of mortmain. It is always guarded, however, by a very powerful principle, the plain and evident interest of every individual to whom any share of it shall ever belong. No part of it can ever afterwards be employed to maintain any but productive hands, without an evident loss to the person who thus perverts it from its proper destination. The prodigal perverts it in this manner; by not confining his expense with his income, he encroaches upon his capital. Like him who perverts the revenues of some pious foundation to profane purposes, he pays the wages of idleness with those funds which the frugality of his forefathers had, as it were, consecrated to the maintenance of industry. By diminishing the funds destined for the employment of productive labour, he necessarily diminishes, as far as it depends upon him, the quantity of that labour which adds a value to the subject upon which it is bestowed, and, consequently, the value of the annual produce of the land and labour of the whole country, the real wealth and revenue of its inhabitants. If the prodigality of some was not compensated by the frugality of others, the conduct of every prodigal, by feeding the idle with the bread of the industrious, tends not only to beggar himself, but to impoverish his country.

[5, vol. 1 *pp. 337–9*]

DOCUMENT 13   PUBLIC AND PRIVATE BANKS

Written in the aftermath of the commercial crisis of 1825, this extract outlines the security of public banks as opposed to private banks. English banks outside the Bank of England could only attain joint-stock status after legislation was passed in 1826.

The principal causes which produce the ruin of private banks may be stated to be – first, a confusion in their accounts, arising from a bad or relaxed and careless management, so very frequently exhibited in common affairs; but which, in banking, must ever be fatal; secondly, speculations with the capital in the bank; and thirdly, and most frequently, accommodating great houses, either from motives of private friendship, or the temptation of extra banking profits, until they are so involved that they must stand or fall with them. The two great failures which have happened in this part of the country, were Surtees, Burdon, and Co. and the Durham Bank. The first was produced by entering into private speculations with the capital in its hands, and the last by accommodating a great mining company. But with public banks these causes, by which failures are generally produced, cannot exist. In the first place, the vigilant check necessarily kept upon the Accountant, and those who have the charge of the books, which must at all times show, without trouble to the Directors, the state of the company's affairs, prevents the possibility of their getting back or into confusion. In the next place, the Directors could not appropriate the money of the bank to views of private speculation, if they were wishful to do so, as they are a check upon each other. If they were respectable men, they would not attempt it, and if they were not, they would not be there: besides, there is no instance recorded of such a thing. In the third place, they have too little personal interest in the bank to be tempted by extra profit out of the path of safety, in accommodating great houses: or if any of them were influenced by private friendship to do so, it could never be the case with them all; and they would be also in that respect a check upon each other.

Thomas Joplin, *An Essay on the General Principles and Present Practice of Banking in England and Scotland,* 6th edn 1827 [9, *pp.* 76–7].

DOCUMENT 14   PROTECTIONISM AND FREE TRADE: A PETITION OF THE LONDON MERCHANTS FOR FREEDOM OF TRADE, 1820

The relative merits of free trade and protectionist tariffs had been debated since the publication of The Wealth of Nations *(1776); but the advocates of free trade only began to influence government economic thinking gradually after 1815. This document argues that a restrictive trade policy imposing extra taxes on British consumers should be abandoned to allow British commodity production to compete in open markets.*

To the Honourable the Commons of Great Britain and Ireland:
The Petition of, etc.
Humbly showeth.

That foreign commerce is eminently conducive to the wealth and prosperity of a country, by enabling it to import the commodities for the production of which the soil, climate, capital and industry of other countries are best calculated, and to export in payment those articles for which its own situation is better adapted.

That freedom from restraint is calculated to give the utmost extension to foreign trade, and the best direction to the capital and industry of the country.

That the maxim of buying in the cheapest market, and selling in the dearest, which regulates every merchant in his individual dealings, is strictly applicable as the best rule for the trade of the whole nation.

That a policy founded on these principles would render the commerce of the world an interchange of mutual advantages, and diffuse an increase of wealth and enjoyments among the inhabitants of each State.

That, unfortunately, a policy the very reverse of this has been, and is, more or less, adopted and acted upon by the Government of this and every other country, each trying to exclude the productions of other countries, with the specious and well meant design of encouraging its own productions, thus inflicting on the bulk of its subjects who are consumers, the necessity of submitting to privations in the quantity or quality of commodities, and thus rendering what ought to be the source of mutual benefit and of harmony among States, a constantly recurring occasion of jealousy and hostility.

That the prevailing prejudices in favour of the protective or restrictive system may be traced to the erroneous supposition that every importation of foreign commodities occasions a diminution or discouragement of our own productions to the same extent, whereas it may be clearly shown that although the particular description of production which could not stand against unrestrained foreign competition would be discouraged, yet as no importation could be continued for any length of time without a corresponding exportation, direct or indirect, there would be an encouragement, for the purpose of that exportation, of some other production to which our situation might be better suited, thus affording at least an equal and probably a greater, and certainly a more beneficial employment to our own capital and labour.

That, of the numerous protective and prohibitory duties of our commercial code, it may be proved, that while all operate as a very heavy tax on the community at large, very few are of any ultimate benefit to the classes in whose favour they were originally instituted, and none to the extent of the loss occasioned by them to other classes.

That, among the other evils of the restrictive or protective system, not the least is, that the artificial protection of one branch of industry, or source of production, against foreign competition, is set up as a ground of claim by other branches for similar protection, so that if the reasoning upon which these restrictive or prohibitory regulations are founded were followed out consistently, it would not stop short of excluding us from all foreign commerce whatsoever. And the same train of argument, which, with corresponding prohibitions and protective duties, should exclude us from foreign trade, might be brought forward to justify the re-enactment of restrictions upon the interchange of productions (unconnected with public revenue) among the kingdoms composing the union, or among the counties of the same kingdom.

That an investigation of the effects of the restrictive system, at this time, is peculiarly called for, as it may, in the opinion of your petitioners, lead to a strong presumption that the distress which now so generally prevails is considerably aggravated by that system, and that some relief may be obtained by the earliest practicable removal of such of the restraints as may be shown to be most injurious to the capital and industry of the community, and to be attended with no compensating benefit to the public revenue.

Your petitioners therefore humbly pray that your honourable house will be pleased to take the subject into consideration, and to adopt such measure as may be calculated to give greater freedom to foreign commerce, and thereby to increase the resources of the State.

[14, *pp. 29–30*]

DOCUMENT 15   **LIVERPOOL**

A contemporary insight into the importance of Liverpool's trade, commerce and docks in the economic life of the early Industrial Revolution.

Liverpool for Situation is the first, for its Trade the second, and for Populousness the fourth Town in the Kingdom. Finely situated on a level Ground on the Banks of the Mersey but a few Miles from the Irish Sea of which we have a scanty Prospect thro the Mouth of the River. The noble Docks in this Port so admirably calculated for the reception of 3 or 4000 Ships, which may lie with perfect ease and Safety afloat; the keys for the Discharge of their Cargoes; the dry Docks for Careening them; the Expedition with which they may put to Sea, give it superior Advantages to any other Port. The only inconvenience is that the Harbour is larboard and there is not always sufficient Water for deep Vessels; so that these are sometimes detained till a Spring Tide when if the wind be unfavourable they cannot depart.

The Town itself is dirty, irregular, illy paved, and in general but indifferently built, though there be some good Streets and Squares. Liverpool being the Port for shipping of the Manufacturies of Manchester, Warrington and other Manufacturing Towns in the Neighbourhood, being concerned largely in the West India Trade, in the Greenland Fisheries, and more largely in the infamous African Trade than any other Place in England occasion a great Forrest of Shipping to be continually in Port. There are several noble institutions for the Poor, the Hospitals, Workhouses &c. The Merchants here are enterprizing and public Spirited which gives great Life and Vigour to the Town, and it is in a State as flourishing as almost any place in Great Britain.

Travel Journal of Jabez Fisher, 1778 [12, *p. 232*].

DOCUMENT 16   CIRCULAR LETTER BY FARELL AND JONES
                OF BRISTOL TO SIXTEEN MERCANTILE
                CORRESPONDENTS IN VIRGINIA,
                10 AUGUST 1770

An explanation of the credit terms offered by a Bristol firm in the Chesapeake trade. Such letters spelled out the length of credit, the interest charges and the procedures for recovering debts when, as here, pressure from other firms caused an alteration in business arrangements.

As we find that the Merchants in general of London Liverpool etc. do now purchase their Goods [for American correspondents] at 12 Months Credit and that it would be more agreeable to our [mercantile] Friends in Virginia if we did the same we have determined to conform thereto and take this Opportunity to inform you the Terms on which we propose doing Business in future with you and our other [mercantile] Correspondents to prevent any mistakes between us viz. We will purchase Goods [ordered by you] at twelve Months Credit and allow you the same [length of credit]. If we are not in Cash [received from you] at the End of twelve Months we are to charge Interest whilst in advance after the rate of five p[er] Cent p[er] Annum[;] if you remit ready Money or [commodities] before the [payments for] the Goods are due we will allow you a Discount thereon after the same Rate[,] the full Remittance to be made by you once a Year [that is, by year's end] or sooner if agreeable to you either in Bills or Tobacco[,] if in the latter we will give you Credit for the freight charged on your Goods by our own ships to the Amount of the nett Proceeds of your Tobacco, but for what we may happen to ship on other Peoples Vessels we can make no Allowance as we must pay the freight out of our own Pockets and of course it would take away the whole of our Commissions. And lastly as we have sometimes been obliged to pay an Attorney [in Virginia] five p[er] Cent to recover Debts from Gentlemen when they drop Correspondence with us besides losing Interest thereon from the time the Debt is paid in Virginia to the times the Bills become due here frequently five or six Months – therefore whenever a Gentleman declines Correspondence with us, he is to pay the Balance of Account into our Compting House with Interest thereon to the time we are in Cash here free from all Charges as we may be put to in recovering the same – We dare say you will think these terms just and reasonable on both sides and if you choose to continue your Correspondence with us thereon we entreat you will sign your Consent at the foot hereof for Mr. Evans to transmitt to us and keep a Duplicate – signed by us in order to prevent any Mistakes on either side in this respect at least in future Correspondence.

Transcribed in Jacob M. Price, *Capital and Credit in British Overseas Trade: The View from the Chesapeake 1700–1776*, Harvard University Press, 1980, pp. 156–7.

DOCUMENT 17   THE COSTS OF RIVER NAVIGATION

Compares the expenses of navigating a barge and a lighter on an unimproved stretch of the River Thames with the costs of the same haulage after projected pound locks and towpaths are installed. The document illustrates the extensive use of hired labour and horses in travelling upstream.

Estimates for the Cost of Working Barges by bow-haling by men and horses c. 1770
Oxford to Mapledurham near Reading
An Account of the Supposed present Expences of a Barge of 110 Tons and a Lighter of 50 Tons therewith being the mode they are usually navigated from Oxford to London and back so far as concerns the Expences between Oxford and Mapledurham.

	£	s.	d.
Downwards			
Six Service Men on board from Oxford to Mapledurham 2 days each being 34 Miles at 4s. A Day each for their wages and provisions.	2	8	0
NB. These Mens wages are generally paid by the voyage but they would average above			
Upwards			
40 Hirelings or men to Tow from Mapledurham to Days Lock 17¾ Miles – 2 days at 5s. Each for wages only – being the price commonly paid	10	0	0
Provisions and Beer for said 40 Men at 1s. A day each including 4d. each for one nights quarters	4	0	0
10 Horses from Days Lock to Sutton 6¾ & Carter	2	15	0
40 Men to Culham 2 miles at 1s. each	2	0	0
40 Hirelings or Towers from Culham to Oxford as far as towed by men at 2s. 6d. each	5	0	0
6 Horses also used with the men at 5s. each	1	12	0
Hire of Cable at 8 Locks at 3s. 6d. each	1	8	0
6 Service men 4 days from Mapledurham to Oxford at 4s. a day each for wages and provisions	4	16	0
Tolls of the present Locks and Winches at about 1s. 8d. a ton on 160 Tons Greatboat & Lighter	13	6	8
NB. Some of the Tolls are paid by the Barge – some by the year – and some by each horse passing	47	5	8
	43	10	8

Saving Each Voyage by the improved State and also the
safety, certainty and dispatch – and if the trade increased
the savings will be greater

3   15   0

An Account of the probable expences of a Barge of 110
Tons and a Lighter of 50 Tons navigated from Oxford
to Mapledurham (in the way to London) and back
on a supposition that Eight new Pound Locks were erected
and a Horse towing path made according to the improvements
below Mapledurham.

	£.	s.	d.
Downwards			
Four Service men on board from Oxford to Mapledurham 2 days at 4d. each a Day	1	12	0

Upwards
10 Horses 34 Miles and Carter at 4d. a Mile being the full
price of postchaise horses and nearly the Average Expence
of towing in the improved part of the river

5   13   4

Or the Horses may be reckon'd by the day 10 horses 2 days
at 5s. A day each & 3s. a day for the Carter amount to
£5 6s. 0d.

There are a set of as many horses let at Marlow to Tow the
Barges to the Kennet which is ¾ of the above Distance and
through 6 pound Locks those are charged £3 6s. 0d. so that
according to this the Horses would come only to £4 19s. 0d.

Additional or New Tolls to be paid at the 8 New pound Locks
at 4d. a ton at Each or 2s. 8d. in the whole on 160 Tons
Greatboat and Lighter

21   6   8

4 Service Men two days from Mapledurham to Oxford at
4s. a day each Wages and provisions

1   12   0

Tolls of the Old Locks and Winches as on the other side
though it is presumed several of the payments for the
Horses towing as at present would cease – and in the improved
state the Boats would last much longer – and not be liable to
the Dangers and delays at present

13   6   8
—————
43   10   8

Reprinted in Mary Prior, *Fisher Row: Fishermen, Bargemen, and Canal Boatmen in Oxford, 1500–1900*, Oxford University Press, 1982, pp. 364–5.

DOCUMENT 18   CANALS

An early accounrt of the benefits accruing from the construction of canals in industrial areas.

... As soon therefore as it appeared, that an easy and commodious Passage could be opened between Manchester and Liverpool, all Diffidence and all Difficulties vanished. Surveys were immediately directed; and, as soon as they were perfected, Subscriptions chearfully followed, the Nobility and Gentry expressing the warmest Zeal in risquing their Private Property for the public Service. But then this Zeal was according to Knowledge; they were clearly convinced of the Utility of the Undertaking; and they saw without suffering any Uneasiness, that Time, Labour, and Expence, must purchase them those Benefits this new Navigation was to bestow, and therefore what in Days of less Industry, less Commercial Spirit, and, let us add, less Opulence, would have been held insuperable Obstacles, did not at all deter them from pursuing so great and so glorious a Design.

WHAT the actual Advantages that will be derived from these Canals when finished, may be, Time and Experience only can determine; but upon what reasonable Expectations they have been so steadily as well as strenuously supported, is incumbent upon me to report, in order to justify the Pains taken about them in this Work. It is a vast Tract of Country through which they are to pass, and not barely one or two, but several Counties that are to share the Benefit of them, with this remarkable Circumstance in their Favour, that in no Part of this noble Island could such a Communication be of more Use, the Number considered of large, and many of them manufacturing Towns, in its Vicinity. All Kinds of Provisions, but more especially Grain, will by their means be rendered cheaper, and kept to a more equal Price. For by furnishing Manure from great Distances at a low Rate, and giving a quick Carriage even to remote Markets, the Canal will excite an active Spirit of Cultivation, and the Certainty of obtaining a speedy Supply at a small Expence will render an unreasonable Rise of Corn, where it has been in Times past frequently and fatally experienced, for the future in a great measure impracticable. Many bulky, but at the same time very useful Commodities, such as Flint, Free, Lime, Mill, Grinding, and Paving Stones, Marl, Slate, Coals of different Kinds, Marble, Alabaster, Iron Ore, will find a much easier and cheaper Passage, and of course reach many more and those too better Markets, than they can be carried to, circumstances as they are at present.

FREQUENT Additions will probably be made to these natural Riches from the Discoveries that must arise from the cutting through a Variety of Soils in the Progress of this great Work, some Instances of which have occurred already. Besides, the Staples of these several Counties may be carried farther, in great Quantities, and be notwithstanding afforded at lower Rates, such as Timber from different Parts of Lancashire, the Salt and Cheese of Cheshire, Earthen-ware from Staffordshire, numerous Articles from Birmingham, and all the various Manufactures from Manchester and other Places, will be relieved from a Variety of Impediments under which they have hitherto laboured. Raw Materials of every Sort will be conveyed with much more Ease and Expedition to the several Towns where they are wrought up, and, when manufactured, will with like Facility be carried to the Ports from which they are usually shipped, either Coast-ways to different Parts of this, or into other Countries. Thus Agriculture, Manufactures, domestic Trade, foreign Commerce and every Species of Industry subservient to all these, will be evidently and in a high Degree promoted by this Inland Navigation, to say nothing of the Numbers who will live and be comfortably subsisted by it ...

John Campbell, *A Political Survey of Britain*, 1774, in D. B. Horn and Mary Ransome (eds), *English Historical Documents 1714–1783*, London, 1957, pp. 547–8.

DOCUMENT 19   THE INCREASE IN ROAD TRAFFIC

Relates the growth of long-distance road traffic from Leicester to the need for heavy goods haulage in the Industrial Revolution, something replicated throughout England. In this instance the growth in road traffic is linked specifically to the hosiery industry of the east Midlands.

About half a century ago, the heavy goods passing through Leicester for London to the South, and on to the Great Northern Lines to Leeds and Manchester did not require more than about one daily broad-wheeled waggon each way. These ... were also fully adequate for the supply and transit of goods for all the intermediate towns, of course including Leicester. One weekly waggon, to and fro, served Coventry, Warwick, Birmingham, and on to Bristol and the West of England; the return waggon being capable of bringing all from that quarter that was directed to Leicester, and all the Northern and North-Eastern districts beyond, At present there are about two waggons, two caravans, and two fly-boats, daily passing or starting from Leicester for London and its intermediate towns: the same number ... extend the connection not only to Leeds and Manchester, but by means of canal conveyance to the ports of Liverpool and Hull. There are at least six weekly waggons to Birmingham, independent of those to Bristol three times a week, and the same to Stamford, Cambridge, Wisbeach, and the Eastern counties; to Nottingham to the same extent, exclusive of carts; and at least two hundered and fifty country carriers to and from the villages, many twice a week, necessary to keep up the conveyance of materials and manufactured goods between the workmen and the hosiers, and the wholesale and retail dealers in other articles of necessity ...

Richard Phillips, *A Personal Tour through the United Kingdom*, 1828 [14, p. 45].

DOCUMENT 20   THE SUCCESS OF THE LIVERPOOL –
MANCHESTER LINE

The Liverpool to Manchester railway, opened in 1830, was the first successful railway line to operate between large cities in the industrial heartland of Britain. This extract points out the importance of passenger traffic in generating profits for the investors.

The great success attending this splendid work being in a principal degree attributable to the passengers conveyed by it, the chief inducement thenceforward to embark in similar undertakings has been the number of travellers and not the amount of goods to be conveyed. Hitherto it has been found, in nearly every case where a railroad adapted for carrying passengers has been brought into operation, that the amount of travelling between the two extremities of the line has been quadrupled. In the case of the Liverpool and Manchester Railway, the income derived from this source has enabled the Company to meet a large amount of extraordinary expenses, and to divide regularly 10 per cent annually upon the capital, although the outlay in the construction of the work has been more than double the sum contemplated in the original estimates.

G.R. Porter, *The Progress of the Nation*, 1838, p. 65.

DOCUMENT 21   COMPARATIVE TRAVEL COSTS, 1844

These figures, which could be duplicated by other examples, indicate the gains in travel costs by passengers taking canal boats and locomotives rather than stage coaches, while illustrating the slowness of travel on the waterways.

		£	s	d
By Canal boat, Manchester to London				
2 adults' passage, 14s. each		1	8	0
3 children's passage, 7s. each		1	1	0
Provisions, etc. for 5 days' passage, 5s. each		1	5	0
	Total	3	14	0
By Coach, Manchester to London, 186 miles [297.6 km]				
2 adults' passage, 30s. each		3	0	0
3 children's passage, 15s. each		2	5	0
Coachmen and Guard			7	0
Food etc.			10	0
	Total	6	2	0

By Railway, Manchester to London, 212 miles [339.2 km]
Third-class, Manchester to Birmingham,

2 adults' passage, 11s. each		1	2	0
3 children's passage, 5s. 6d. each			16	6
Third-class, Birmingham to London,				
2 adults' passage, 14s. each		1	8	0
3 children's passage, 7s. each		1	1	0
Food etc., 1s. 6d. each			7	6
	Total	4	15	0

Report of Select Committee on Railways, 1844, Appendix no. 4, *Parliamentary Papers*.

GLOSSARY

Back-projection an essential tool used by modern demographers, consisting of successively back-dating and revising the known age structure of a census, thus deriving earlier 'censuses' at five-year intervals. An important way of reconstructing the size and age structure of past populations.

Capitalism this term can refer to possessing capital, or wealth, used in the manufacturing of goods. It also refers to the social system based on this method of production and to the systematic pursuit of profit in a market economy, often by *entrepreneurs*.

Circulating capital funds embodied in stocks of raw material and work in progress (e.g. semi-finished goods, credit) as opposed to fixed assets.

Common rights an aspect of manorial custom which defined common rights and copyhold privileges for landholders of all classes. These customary rights stemmed from immemorial practice. Most importantly, common rights included common of pasture, but they also covered many other customary privileges, such as the right to glean harvested fields, the burning of furze for ashes, and rights to fish or capture game.

Comparative advantage a theorem that advocates free trade in nearly every circumstance. Person, country or region A may produce goods X and Y with less cost than person, country or region B. Nevertheless, market forces caused by free trade will encourage specialization, where A will produce only one good, leaving B to produce the other. By doing so, the joint output will be larger than if both A and B pursued a diversified production strategy.

Demand the amount of goods that consumers are prepared to buy at a given time at a particular price. Purchasers typically will desire more goods or services as the prices for those items fall.

Demography the study of the history of population growth and decline.

Economic growth   the process of increasing productive capacity in the economy, and thus a means of increasing national income. The increase in value of goods and services produced in the economy in year 2 over year 1 is calculated as a percentage of the value of production in year 1 to give the *rate of economic growth* (a central measure of economic performance).

Economies of scale   the cost savings gained by enlarging the size of a firm, a process or an industry. These economies are achieved mainly through opportunities for specialisation.

Elasticity, demand   the responsiveness of the quantity of goods demanded to a change in the price of a good.

Elasticity, supply   the responsiveness of the quantity of goods supplied by producers to a change in the price of a good.

Entail   a legal device whereby land was settled on a number of persons in succession, so that it could not be dealt with by any one possessor as absolute owner.

Entrepreneur   one who undertakes the risk of starting a new venture or expanding an old one and also normally assumes responsibility for administering the project.

Factor of production   a resource used in producing final goods and services, usually placed in one of four main categories – land, labour, capital and entrepreneurial ability.

Family reconstitution   the systematic assemblage and articulation of information about the life histories of families, starting with data on birth or baptism, marriage and death and then adding as much additional data as is needed (on, for instance, occupations, residence, social status, income and/or wealth).

Fertility   the incidence of live births in a specified population.

Fixed capital   capital invested in durable goods such as buildings, plant and machinery.

Free trade   the absence of protective tariffs or other restraints on trade.

Inflation   a rise in the average level of prices; a fall in the value (purchasing power) of money.

Joint-stock banks   privately owned banks receiving deposits and making loans through a large number of branches, in which the capital is divided into small units allowing a number of investors to contribute varying amounts of the total. Profits were divided among stockholders in proportion to the number of shares they owned.

Mortality   the incidence of deaths in a specified population.

Multiplier effect   typically refers to the sequence of events where an expenditure, or 'injection', of one unit spending is subsequently respent many times over as the money passes through the economy. The result is an increase in the national income by a factor that is larger than the initial expenditure.

National Debt   the total outstanding borrowings of the central government Exchequer, consisting of funded debt, floating debt such as short-term borrowings, and other unfunded debt.

National income   a basic concept of macro-economics, referring to the money value of the total amount of goods and services produced in the economy over a stated period, usually a year, and to the total of all incomes earned over the same period. Also known as Gross National Product (GNP), which includes income from foreign investments by British residents but excludes net income paid to foreign holders of British investments. Gross Domestic Product (GDP) omits both these types of income.

Nuptiality   the rate of marriage in a given population.

Primogeniture   inheritance by the eldest male son.

Productivity   a measure of the flow of output from the use of given amounts of factors of production (i.e. land, capital, labour). It can be expressed differently as the measure of the efficiency of inputs to a productive process.

Social savings   the benefit from a project, measured to include all benefits over the entire society. The annual social savings divided by the opportunity cost of the investment would be the social rate of return.

Strict settlement   a legal term referring to land settled by a limitation to the parent for life and after his death to his first and other sons in succession.

Supply   the amount of goods that producers and distributors are prepared to sell at a given time at a particular price. Suppliers typically will provide more goods or services as prices for those items rise.

Transaction costs   the expenses of doing business, such as the expense of finding someone to do it with, of negotiating a deal, and of ensuring the deal is carried out.

Wages   the price paid for the use of labour. *Money wages* are the amount of money received by a worker per unit of time. *Real wages* are the quantity of goods and services that can be obtained with money wages.

BIBLIOGRAPHY

CUP = Cambridge University Press
EcHR = *Economic History Review*, 2nd series
EEH = *Explorations in Economic History*
EHR = *English Historical Review*
HJ = *Historical Journal*
JEcH = *Journal of Economic History*
JTH = *Journal of Transport History*
LUP = Liverpool University Press
MUP = Manchester University Press
OUP = Oxford University Press
PP = *Past and Present*

PRINTED PRIMARY SOURCES

1   Anderson, B. L. and Cottrell, P. L. (eds), *Money and Banking in England: The Development of the Banking System, 1694–1914,* David & Charles, 1974.

2   Ashton, T. S. (ed.), *An Eighteenth-Century Industrialist: Peter Stubs of Warrington, 1756–1806,* MUP, 1939.

3   Bland, A. E., Brown, P. A. and Tawney, R. H. (eds*), English Economic History: Select Documents,* Bell, 1914.

4   Caird, J., *English Agriculture in 1850 and 1851,* reprinted Cass, 1968.

5   Campbell, R. H. and Skinner, A. S. (eds), *Adam Smith: An Enquiry into the Nature and Causes of the Wealth of Nations,* 2 vols, OUP, 1976.

6   Clapp, B. W. (ed.), *Documents in English Economic History: England since 1760,* Bell, 1976.

7   Elsas, M. (ed.), *Iron in the Making: Dowlais Iron Company Letters, 1782–1860,* Glamorgan County Records Committee, 1960.

8   Flew, A. (ed.), *Thomas Malthus: An Essay on the Principle of Population, and a Summary View of the Principle of Population,* Penguin, 1970.

9   Flinn, M. W. (ed.), *Readings in Economic and Social History*, Macmillan, 1965.

10   Hartwell, R. M. (ed.), *David Ricardo: On the Principles of Political Economy*, Penguin, 1971.

11   Mitchell, B. R. and Deane, P. (eds), *Abstract of British Historical Statistics*, CUP, 1962.

12   Morgan, K. (ed.), *An American Quaker in the British Isles: The Travel Journals of Jabez Maud Fisher, 1775–1779*, OUP, 1992.

13   Paul, E. and C. (eds), *Karl Marx: Capital*, J. M. Dent, 1962.

14   Porter, R. and Royle, E. (eds), *Documents of the Early Industrial Revolution*, Cambridge Local Examinations Syndicate, 1983.

15   Price, J. M. (ed.), *Joshua Johnson's Letterbook, 1771–1774: Letters from a Merchant in London to his Partners in Maryland*, London Record Society, 15, 1979.

SECONDARY SOURCES

General books and articles

16   Ashton, T. S., *An Economic History of England: The Eighteenth Century*, OUP, 1955.

17   Ashton, T. S., *The Industrial Revolution, 1760–1830*, 1948, reprinted OUP, 1996.

18   Berg, M. and Hudson, P., 'Rehabilitating the Industrial Revolution', *EcHR*, 45, 1992.

19   Cannadine, D., 'The present and the past in the English Industrial Revolution, 1880–1980,' *PP*, no. 103, 1984.

20   Crafts, N. F. R., *British Economic Growth during the Industrial Revolution*, OUP, 1985.

21   Daunton, M. J., *Progress and Poverty: An Economic and Social History of Britain, 1700–1850*, OUP, 1995.

22   Deane, P., *The First Industrial Revolution*, 2nd edn, CUP, 1979.

23   Deane, P. and Cole, W. A., *British Economic Growth 1688–1959*, 2nd edn, CUP, 1967.

24   Evans, E. J., *The Forging of the Modern State: Early Industrial Britain*, 2nd edn, Longman, 1995.

25   Flinn, M. W., *The Origins of the Industrial Revolution*, Longman, 1966.

26   Floud, R. C. and McCloskey, D. N. (eds), *The Economic History of Britain since 1700: vol. 1: 1700–1860*, 2nd edn, CUP, 1994.

27   Harley, C. K., 'British industrialisation before 1841: evidence of slower growth during the Industrial Revolution', *JEcH*, 42, 1982.

28   Hartwell, R. M. (ed.), *The Causes of the Industrial Revolution in England*, Methuen, 1967.

29   Hartwell, R. M., *The Industrial Revolution and Economic Growth*, Methuen, 1971.

30   Hobsbawm, E. J., *Industry and Empire*, Penguin, 1968.
31   Hoppit, J., 'Counting the Industrial Revolution', *EcHR*, 43, 1990.
32   Hudson, P., *The Industrial Revolution*, Arnold, 1992.
33   Landes, D. S., *The Unbound Prometheus: Technological Change and Industrial Development in Western Europe from 1750 to the Present*, CUP, 1969.
34   Langton, J. and Morris, R. J. (eds), *Atlas of Industrializing Britain, 1780–1914*, Methuen, 1989.
35   Laslett, P., *The World We Have Lost*, Methuen, 1965.
36   Lee, C. H., *The British Economy since 1700: A Macroeconomic Perspective*, CUP, 1986.
37   Mathias, P., *The Transformation of England: Essays in the Economic and Social History of England in the Eighteenth Century*, Methuen, 1979.
38   Mathias, P., *The First Industrial Nation: An Economic History of Britain 1700–1914*, 2nd edn, Methuen, 1983.
39   Mathias, P. and Davis, J. A. (eds), *The Nature of Industrialization*, 5 vols., Blackwell, 1989–96.
40   McKendrick, N., Brewer, J. and Plumb, J. H., *The Birth of a Consumer Society: The Commercialisation of Eighteenth-Century England*, Hutchinson, 1983.
41   Mokyr, J., 'Demand vs Supply in the Industrial Revolution', *JEcH*, 37, 1977.
42   More, C., *The Industrial Age: Economy and Society in Britain 1750–1985*, 2nd edn, Longman, 1997.
43   O'Brien, P. K. and Quinault, R. (eds), *The Industrial Revolution and British Society*, CUP, 1993.
44   Pawson, E., *The Early Industrial Revolution: Britain in the Eighteenth Century*, Batsford, 1979.
45   Pollard, S., *The Genesis of Modern Management: A Study of the Industrial Revolution in Britain*, Penguin, 1968.
46   Pollard, S., *Peaceful Conquest: The Industrialization of Europe 1760–1970*, OUP, 1981.
47   Rostow, W. W. (ed.), *The Economics of Take-Off into Sustained Growth*, Macmillan, 1963.
48   Rostow, W. W., *The Stages of Economic Growth: A Non-Communist Manifesto*, 2nd edn, CUP, 1971.
49   Rule, J., *The Labouring Classes in Early Industrial England, 1750–1850*, Longman, 1986.
50   Rule, J., *The Vital Century: England's Developing Economy 1714–1815*, Longman, 1992.
51   Smout, T. C., *A History of the Scottish People, 1560–1830*, Collins, 1969.
52   Thompson, E. P., *The Making of the English Working Class*, Penguin, 1963.
53   Thompson, E. P., *Customs in Common*, Penguin, 1992.

54 Valenze, D., *The First Industrial Woman*, OUP, 1995.
55 Whatley, C. A., *The Industrial Revolution in Scotland*, CUP, 1997.
56 Wrigley, E. A., *People, Cities and Wealth*, Blackwell, 1987.
57 Wrigley, E. A., *Continuity, Chance and Change: The Character of the Industrial Revolution in England*, CUP, 1988.

Note: To help the reader, detailed studies are listed below under individual chapter headings. Some items, of course, are useful for more than one chapter. In particular, some of the material cited for chapter 4 could also have been listed under chapter 5 and vice versa.

Chapter 2 Population Growth

58 Anderson, M., *Family Structure in Nineteenth Century Lancashire* , CUP, 1971.
59 Anderson, M., *Population Change in North Western Europe, 1750–1850*, Macmillan, 1988.
60 Flinn, M. W. *et al*, *Scottish Population History from the Seventeenth Century to the 1930s* , CUP, 1977.
61 Floud, R. C., Wachter, K. and Gregory, A., *Height, Health and History: Nutritional Status in the United Kingdom, 1750–1980* , CUP, 1990.
62 McKeown, T., *The Modern Rise of Population* , Arnold, 1976.
63 Porter, R., *Disease, Medicine, and Society in England*, 2nd edn, CUP, 1995.
64 Shorter, E., *The Making of the Modern Family*, Fontana, 1977.
65 Tranter, N. L., *Population and Society in England, 1750–1940*, Longman, 1985.
66 Woods, R., 'Population growth and economic change in the eighteenth and nineteenth centuries' in Mathias, P. and Davis, J. A. (eds), *The Nature of Industrialization: The First Industrial Revolutions*, Blackwell, 1989.
67 Woods, R., *The Population of Britain in the Nineteenth Century*, CUP, 1992.
68 Wrigley, E. A. and Schofield, R. S., *The Population History of England, 1541–1871: A Reconstruction*, CUP, 1981.
69 Wrigley, E. A., Davies, R. S., Oeppen, J. E. and Schofield, R. S., *English Population History from Family Reconstitution 1580–1837*, CUP, 1997.

Chapter 3 Agriculture

70 Allen, R. C., *Enclosure and the Yeoman: The Agricultural Development of the South Midlands, 1450–1850*, OUP, 1992.
71 Beckett, J. V., 'The Pattern of Landownership in England and Wales, 1660–1880,' *EcHR*, 37, 1984.
72 Beckett, J. V., *The Agricultural Revolution*, Blackwell, 1990.

73   Brenner, R., 'Agrarian class structure and economic development in pre-industrial Europe', *PP*, no. 70, 1976.

74   Chambers, J. D., 'Enclosure and labour supply in the Industrial Revolution' reprinted in Jones, E. L. (ed.), *Agriculture and Economic Growth in England, 1650–1815*, Methuen, 1967.

75   Chambers, J. D. and Mingay, G. E., *The Agricultural Revolution, 1750–1880*, Batsford, 1966.

76   Crafts, N.F.R., 'Enclosure and labour supply revisited', *EEH*, 15, 1978.

77   Habbakuk, H. J., *Marriage, Debt and the Estates System: English Landownership, 1650–1950*, OUP, 1994.

78   Hammond, J. L. and B., *The Village Labourer 1760–1832: A Study in the Government of England before the Reform Bill*, 1911, 4th edn reprinted Longman, 1978.

79   Holderness, B. A., 'Prices, productivity and output' in Mingay, G. E. (ed.), *The Agrarian History of England and Wales, vol. 6: 1750–1850*, CUP, 1989.

80   Humphries, J., 'Enclosures, common right and women: the proletarianisation of families in the later eighteenth and early nineteenth centuries', *JEcH*, 50, 1990.

81   Jackson, R. V., 'Growth and deceleration in English agriculture, 1660–1790,' *EcHR*, 38, 1985.

82   Kerridge, E., *The Agricultural Revolution*, Allen and Unwin, 1967.

83   King, P., 'Customary rights and women's earnings: the importance of gleaning to the rural labouring poor, 1750–1850', *EcHR*, 44, 1991.

84   Kussmaul, A., *A General View of the Rural Economy of England, 1538–1840*, CUP, 1990.

85   Mingay, G. E. (ed.), *The Agrarian History of England and Wales, vol. vi: 1750–1850*, CUP, 1989.

86   Mingay, G. E., *Parliamentary Enclosure in England: An Introduction to its Causes, Incidence and Impact, 1750–1850*, Longman, 1997.

87   Neeson, J. M., *Commons: Common Right, Enclosure and Social Change in England, 1700–1820*, CUP, 1993.

88   O'Brien, P. K., 'Agriculture and the home market for English industry, 1660–1820', *EHR*, 100, 1985.

89   Overton, M., *Agricultural Revolution in England: The Transformation of the Agrarian Economy, 1500–1850*, CUP, 1996.

90   Snell, K. D. M., *Annals of the Labouring Poor*, CUP, 1985.

91   Thompson, F. M. L., *English Landed Society in the Nineteenth Century*, Routledge & Kegan Paul, 1963.

92   Thompson, F. M. L., 'The second Agricultural Revolution, 1815–1880', *EcHR*, 21, 1968.

93   Turner, M., *Enclosures in Britain, 1750–1830*, Macmillan, 1984.

94   Turner, M., *English Parliamentary Enclosure: Its Historical Geography and Economic History*, Dawson, 1980.

95   Wells, R., *Wretched Faces: Famine in Wartime England, 1793–1801*, Alan Sutton, 1988.

96   Wordie, J. R., 'The chronology of English enclosures, 1500–1914', *EcHR*, 36, 1983.

Chapter 4 Domestic Industry and Proto-Industrialization

97   Berg, M., Hudson, P., and Sonenscher, M. (eds), *Manufacture in Town and Country before the Factory*, CUP, 1983.
98   Berg, M., 'Women's work, mechanisation and the early phases of industrialisation in England' in Joyce, P. (ed.), *The Historical Meanings of Work*, CUP, 1987.
99   Berg, M., *The Age of Manufactures, 1700–1820: Industry, Innovation and Work in Britain*, 2nd edn, Routledge, 1994.
100 Bythell, D., *The Handloom Weavers: A Study in the English Cotton Industry during the Industrial Revolution*, CUP, 1969.
101 Bythell, D., *The Sweated Trades: Outwork in Nineteenth-Century Britain*, Batsford, 1978.
102 Bythell, D., 'Women in the workforce' in O'Brien, P. K. and Quinault, R. (eds), *The Industrial Revolution and British Society*, CUP, 1993.
103 Clarkson, L. A., *Proto-Industrialisation: The First Phase of Industrialisation?*, Macmillan, 1985.
104 Coleman, D. C., 'Proto-industrialisation: a concept too many', *EcHR*, 36, 1983, reprinted in his *Myth, History and the Industrial Revolution*, Hambledon, 1992.
105 Corfield, P. J., *The Impact of English Towns, 1700–1800*, OUP, 1982.
106 Horrell, S. and Humphries, J., 'Women's labour force participation and the transition to the male breadwinner family, 1790–1865', *EcHR*, 48, 1995.
107 Houston, R. A. and Snell, K. D. M., 'Proto-industrialisation? Cottage industry, social change, and Industrial Revolution', *HJ*, 27, 1984.
108 Hudson, P., *The Genesis of Industrial Capital: A Study of the West Riding Wool Textile Industry c. 1750–1850*, CUP, 1986.
109 Hudson, P. (ed.), *Regions and Industries: A Perspective on the Industrial Revolution in Britain*, CUP, 1989.
110 Hunt, E. H., *British Labour History, 1815–1914*, Weidenfeld and Nicolson, 1981.
111 John, A. V. (ed.), *Unequal Opportunities: Women's Employment in England 1800–1918*, Blackwell, 1986.
112 Levine, D., *Family Formation in an Age of Nascent Capitalism*, Academic Press, 1977.
113 Levine, D., 'Industrialization and the proletarian family in England', *PP*, no. 107, 1985.
114 Malcolmson, R. W., *Life and Labour in England 1700–1780*, Hutchinson, 1981.
115 Medick, H., 'The proto-industrial family economy: the structural function of household and family during the transition from peasant to industrial capitalism', *Social History*, 1, 1976.

116 Mendels, F. F., 'Proto-industrialisation: the first phase of the industrialisation process', *JEcH*, 32, 1972.

117 Osterud, N. G., 'Gender divisions and the organisation of work in the Leicester hosiery industry' in John, A. V. (ed.), *Unequal Opportunities: Women's Employment in England 1800–1918*, Blackwell, 1986.

118 Pinchbeck, I., *Women Workers and the Industrial Revolution*, 1930, reprinted Cass, 1969.

119 Rendall, J., *Women in Industrializing Society: England 1750–1880*, Blackwell, 1990.

120 Richards, E., 'Women and the British economy since about 1700: an interpretation', *History*, 59, 1974.

121 Styles, J., 'Manufacturing, consumption and design in eighteenth-century England' in Brewer, J. and Porter, R. (eds), *Consumption and the World of Goods*, Routledge, 1993.

Chapter 5 Factory Production and the Textile Industries

122 Chapman, S. D., *The Early Factory Masters*, David & Charles, 1967.

123 Chapman, S. D., *The Cotton Industry and the Industrial Revolution*, 2nd edn, Macmillan, 1987.

124 Court, W. H. B., *The Rise of the Midland Industries, 1600–1838*, OUP, 1938.

125 Cunningham, H., 'The employment and unemployment of children in England, c.1680–1851,' *PP*, no. 126, 1990.

126 Dinwiddy, J. R., *Radicalism and Reform in Britain, 1780–1850*, Hambledon, 1992.

127 Edwards, M. M., *The Growth of the British Cotton Trade, 1780–1815*, MUP, 1967.

128 Farnie, D. A., *The English Cotton Industry and the World Market 1815–1896*, OUP, 1979.

129 Fitton, R. S. and Wadsworth, A. P., *The Strutts and the Arkwrights, 1758–1830*, MUP, 1958.

130 Hall, C., 'The world turned upside down? The working class family in cotton textiles, 1780–1850' in E. Whitelegg (ed.), *The Changing Experience of Women*, Martin Robertson, 1982.

131 Hopkins, E., 'Working hours and conditions during the industrial revolution: a reappraisal', *EcHR*, 35, 1982.

132 Hopkins, E., *Birmingham: The First Manufacturing Town in the World*, Weidenfeld and Nicolson, 1989.

133 Jenkins, D. T. and Ponting, K. G., *The British Wool Textile Industry, 1770–1914*, Heinemann, 1982.

134 Jeremy, D. J., *Transatlantic Industrial Revolution: The Diffusion of Textile Technologies between Britain and America, 1790–1830*, Blackwell, 1981.

135 John, A. H., *The Industrial Development of South Wales 1750–1850: An Essay*, University of Wales Press, 1950.

136 Lemire, B., *Fashion's Favourite: The Cotton Trade and the Consumer in Britain, 1660–1800*, OUP, 1991.

137 McKendrick, N., 'Josiah Wedgwood and factory discipline', *HJ*, 4, 1961.

138 McKendrick, N., 'Home demand and economic growth: a new view of the role of women and children in the Industrial Revolution' in N. McKendrick (ed.), *Historical Perspectives: Studies in English Thought and Society in honour of J. H. Plumb*, Europa, 1974.

139 Musson, A. E., *The Growth of British Industry*, Batsford, 1978.

140 Pollard, S., 'Factory discipline in the Industrial Revolution', *EcHR*, 16, 1963–64.

141 Randall, A. J., *Before the Luddites: Custom, Community and Machinery in the English Woollen Industry, 1776–1809*, CUP, 1991.

142 Rose, M. B. (ed.), *The Lancashire Cotton Industry: A History since 1700*, Lancashire County Books, 1996.

143 Rule, J., *The Experience of Labour in Eighteenth Century Industry*, Croom Helm, 1981.

144 Wadsworth, A. P. and Mann, J. de L., *The Cotton Trade and Industrial Lancashire, 1600–1780*, MUP, 1931.

145 Wilson, R. G., 'The supremacy of the Yorkshire cloth industry in the eighteenth century' in Harte, N. B. and Ponting, K. G. (eds), *Textile History and Economic History*, MUP, 1973.

Chapter 6 Coal and Iron

146 Church, R. A., *The History of the British Coal Industry, vol iii: 1830–1913: Victorian Pre-eminence*, OUP, 1986.

147 Flinn, M. W., *The History of the British Coal Industry, vol. ii: 1700–1830: The Industrial Revolution*, OUP, 1984.

148 Harris, J. R., *The British Iron Industry, 1700–1850*, Macmillan, 1988.

149 Harris, J. R., 'Skills, coal and British industry in the eighteenth century,' *History*, 61 (1976), reprinted in his *Essays in Industry and Technology in the 18th Century: England and France*, Variorum, 1992.

150 Hyde, C. K., *Technological Change and the British Iron Industry, 1700–1870*, Princeton University Press, 1977.

151 Langton, J., *Geographical Change and Industrial Revolution: Coalmining in south-west Lancashire, 1590-1799*, CUP, 1979.

152 Tweedale, G., *Steel City: Entrepreneurship, Strategy and Technology in Sheffield 1743–1993*, OUP, 1995.

153 von Tunzelmann, G. N., *Steam Power and British Industrialisation to 1860*, OUP, 1978.

Chapter 7 Entrepreneurs, Capital, and Business Enterprise

154 Anderson, B. L., 'The attorney and the capital market in Lancashire' in Harris, J. R. (ed.), *Liverpool and Merseyside: Essays in the Economic and Social History of the Port and its Hinterland*, LUP, 1969.

155 Brewer, J., *The Sinews of Power: War, Money and the English State, 1688–1783*, Hutchinson, 1988.

156 Cameron, R. (ed.), *Banking in the Early Stages of Industrialization: A Study in Comparative Economic History*, OUP, 1967.

157 Checkland, S. G., *Scottish Banking: A History, 1695–1973*, Collins, 1975.

158 Collins, M., *Money and Banking in the U. K.: A History*, Croom Helm, 1988.

159 Cottrell, P. L., *Industrial Finance, 1830–1914: The Finance and Organisation of English Manufacturing Industry*, rev. edn, Methuen, 1983.

160 Crouzet, F. (ed.), *Capital Formation in the Industrial Revolution*, Methuen, 1972.

161 Crouzet, F., *The First Industrialists: The Problem of Origins*, CUP, 1985.

162 Feinstein, C. H., 'Capital formation in Britain' in Mathias, P. and Postan, M. M. (eds), *The Cambridge Economic History of Europe*, vol. 7, Part 1, CUP, 1978.

163 Feinstein, C. H. and Pollard, S. (eds), *Studies in Capital Formation in the United Kingdom, 1750–1920*, OUP, 1988.

164 Honeyman, K., *Origins of Business Enterprise: Business Leadership in the Industrial Revolution*, MUP, 1982.

165 Hoppit, J., 'Financial crises in eighteenth-century England', *EcHR, 39*, 1986.

166 Hoppit, J., *Risk and Failure in English Business, 1700–1800*, CUP, 1987.

167 Jenkins, D. T., *The West Riding Wool Textile Industry, 1770–1835: A Study of Fixed Capital Formation*, Pasold Research Fund, 1975.

168 MacLeod, C., *Inventing the Industrial Revolution*, CUP, 1988.

169 Mathias, P., *The Brewing Industry in England, 1700–1830*, CUP, 1959.

170 Mui, H. C. and L. H., *Shops and Shopkeeping in Eighteenth-Century England*, Routledge, 1989.

171 Neal, L., 'The finance of business during the Industrial Revolution' in Floud, R. C. and McCloskey, D. N. (eds), *The Economic History of Britain since 1700*, 2nd edn, CUP, 1994.

172 O'Brien, P. K., 'Public finance in the wars with France 1793–1815' in H. T. Dickinson (ed.), *Britain and the French Revolution, 1789–1815*, Macmillan, 1989.

173 Pressnell, L. S., *Country Banking in the Industrial Revolution*, OUP, 1956.

174 Styles, J., ' "Our traitorous money makers": the Yorkshire coiners and the law, 1760–83' in Brewer, J. and Styles, J. (eds), *An Ungovernable People: The English and their Law in the Seventeenth and Eighteenth Centuries*, Hutchinson, 1980.

175 Williamson, J. G., *Coping with City Growth during the British Industrial Revolution*, CUP, 1990.

176 Wilson, R. G., *Gentlemen Merchants: The Merchant Community in Leeds, 1700–1830*, MUP, 1971.

Chapter 8 Foreign Trade

177 Cain, P. J. and Hopkins, A. G., *British Imperialism: Innovation and Expansion, 1688–1914*, Longman, 1993.

178 Chapman, S. D., *Merchant Enterprise in Britain: From the Industrial Revolution to the First World War*, CUP, 1992.

179 Crouzet, F., 'Toward an export economy: British exports during the Industrial Revolution', *EEH*, 17, 1980.

180 Davis, R., *The Industrial Revolution and British Overseas Trade* Leicester University Press, 1979.

181 Davis, R., 'English foreign trade, 1700–1774', *EcHR*, 15 (1962), reprinted in Minchinton, W. E. (ed.), *The Growth of English Overseas Trade in the Seventeenth and Eighteenth Centuries*, Methuen, 1969.

182 Devine, T. M., *The Tobacco Lords: A Study of the Tobacco Merchants of Glasgow and their Trading Activities c.1740–90*, John Donald, 1975.

183 Devine, T. M. and Jackson, G. (eds), *Glasgow: Volume 1: Beginnings to 1830*, MUP, 1995.

184 Eversley, D. E. C., 'The Home Market and Economic Growth, 1750–1780' in Jones, E. L. and Mingay, G. E. (eds), *Land, Labour and Population in the Industrial Revolution: Essays presented to J. D. Chambers*, Arnold, 1967.

185 Hyde, F. E., *Liverpool and the Mersey: An Economic History of a Port, 1700–1970*, David & Charles, 1971.

186 Jackson, G., 'The ports' in Aldcroft, D. H. and Freeman, M. J. (eds), *Transport in the Industrial Revolution*, MUP, 1983.

187 Jackson, G., 'The ports' and 'The shipping industry' in Freeman, M. J. and Aldcroft, D. H. (eds), *Transport in Victorian Britain*, MUP, 1988.

188 Langton, J., 'Liverpool and its hinterland in the late eighteenth century' in Anderson, B. L. and Stoney, P. J. M. (eds), *Commerce, Industry and Transport: Studies in Economic Change on Merseyside*, LUP, 1983.

189 Morgan, K., *Bristol and the Atlantic Trade in the Eighteenth Century*, CUP, 1993.

190 Morgan, K., 'Atlantic trade and British economic growth in the Eighteenth century' in Mathias, P. and Davis, J. A. (eds), *The Nature of Industrialization: International Trade and British Economic Growth since the Eighteenth Century*, Blackwell, 1996.

191 O'Brien, P. K. and Engerman, S. L., 'Exports and the growth of the British economy from the Glorious Revolution to the Peace of Ami-

ens' in Solow, B. L. (ed.), *Slavery and the Rise of the Atlantic System*, CUP, 1991.

192 Price, J. M., 'What did merchants do? Reflections on British overseas trade, 1660–1770', *JEcH*, 49, 1989, reprinted in his *Overseas Trade and Traders: Essays on some Commercial, Financial and Political Challenges facing British Atlantic Merchants, 1660–1775*, Variorum, 1996.

193 Richardson, D., 'The slave trade, sugar, and British economic growth, 1748–1776' in Solow, B. L. and Engerman, S. L. (eds), *British Capitalism and Caribbean Slavery: The Legacy of Eric Williams*, CUP, 1987.

194 Williams, E., *Capitalism and Slavery*, Andre Deutsch, 1944.

Chapter 9 Internal Transport

195 Albert, W., *The Turnpike Road System in England, 1663–1840*, CUP, 1972.

196 Albert, W., 'The turnpike trusts' in Aldcroft, D. H. and Freeman, M. J. (eds), *Transport in the Industrial Revolution*, MUP, 1983.

197 Austen, B., 'The impact of the mail coach on public coach services in England and Wales, 1784–1840', *JTH*, 3rd ser., 2, 1981.

198 Bagwell, P. S., *The Transport Revolution from 1770*, Batsford, 1974.

199 Daunton, M. J., *Royal Mail: The Post Office since 1840*, Athlone Press, 1985.

200 Duckham, B. F., 'Canals and river navigations' in Aldcroft, D. H. and Freeman, M. J. (eds), *Transport in the Industrial Revolution*, MUP, 1983.

201 Dyos, H. J. and Aldcroft, D. H., *British Transport: An Economic Survey from the Seventeenth Century to the Twentieth*, Penguin, 1974.

202 Everitt, A., 'Country carriers in the nineteenth century' reprinted in his *Landscape and Community in England*, Hambledon, 1985, ch. 11.

203 Freeman, M. J., 'Road transport in the Industrial Revolution: an interim reassessment', *Journal of Historical Geography*, 6, 1980.

204 Freeman, M. J. and Aldcroft, D. H. (eds), *Transport in Victorian Britain*, MUP, 1988.

205 Gerhold, D., *Road Transport before the Railways: Russell's London Flying Waggons*, CUP, 1993.

206 Gerhold, D., 'Productivity change in road transport before and after Turnpiking, 1690–1840', *EcHR*, 49, 1996.

207 Gourvish, T. R., *Railways and the British Economy 1830–1914*, Macmillan, 1980.

208 Hawke, G. R., *Railways and Economic Growth in England and Wales 1840–1870*, OUP, 1970.

209 Jackman, W. T., *The Development of Transportation in Modern England*, 1916, 3rd edn, Cass, 1966.

210 Kellett, J. R., *The Impact of Railways on Victorian Cities*, Routledge & Kegan Paul, 1969.

211 Pawson, E., *Transport and Economy: The Turnpike Roads of Eighteenth Century Britain*, Academic Press, 1977.

212 Simmons, J., *The Railway in Town and Country, 1830–1914*, David & Charles, 1986.

213 Turnbull, G. L., 'Canals, coal and regional growth during the Industrial Revolution', *EcHR*, 40, 1987.

214 Turnbull, G. L., 'Provincial road carrying in England in the eighteenth century', *JTH*, new ser., 4, 1977.

215 Ward, J. R., *The Finance of Canal Building in Eighteenth Century England*, OUP, 1974.

216 Willan, T. S., *An Eighteenth-Century Shopkeeper: Abraham Dent of Kirkby Stephen*, MUP, 1970.

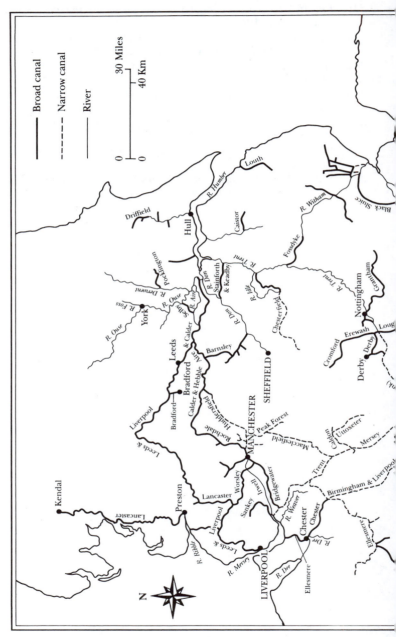

Map 1   The principal waterways of England and Wales c. 1830
Source: John Rule, The Vital Century: England's Developing Economy
1714–1815 (London, 1992), pp. 236–7

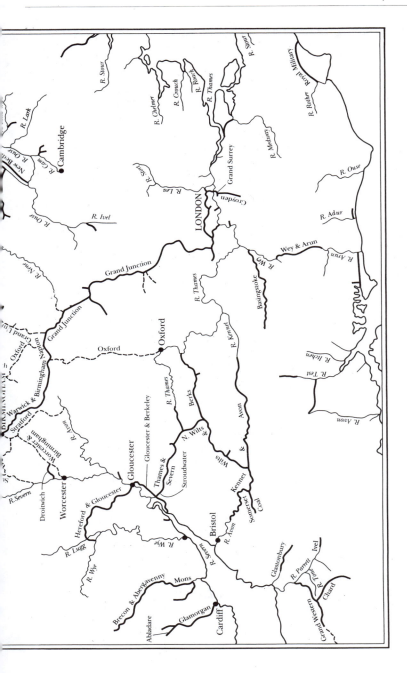

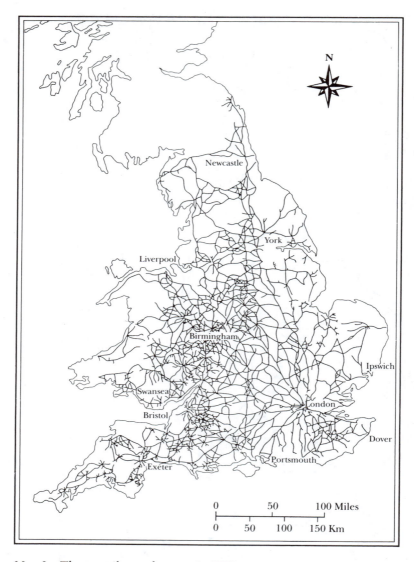

Map 2   The turnpike road system in 1770
Source: John Rule, The Vital Century: England's Developing Economy
1714–1815 (London, 1992), p. 217

INDEX